This book is an amazing insight into the court system and the impact on children when judges make mistakes or do not follow the law. We all would like to believe that mistakes do not happen; however, the reality is that judges do make mistakes and they sometimes do not follow the law. When parents find themselves the recipients of mistakes their recourse is to keep up the costly litigation (parties can have as much justice as they can afford) or file an appeal, which can be a lengthy and costly process. Hopefully this book will help eliminate many mistakes and have an impact on judges to make sure that they follow what they are instructed to follow… THE LAW.

—ATTORNEY CONNIE THACKER, Grand Rapids, MI

Liisa's book is an indispensable resource for parents, attorneys, and judges finding themselves caught up in (often complex and hotly contested) custody and parenting time cases.

As Liisa is an attorney whose practice is predominantly post-divorce custody and parenting time cases, her book is almost a look into "a day in the life of." So often do parents have time with their children shortened or, worse, suspended entirely, on inflammatory motions—oftentimes on an ex parte basis where the targeted parent has no meaningful opportunity to present his or her side of the story. These motions can be brought months, or even years, after a divorce judgment or other order has been finalized (frequently without a trial or significant court-parent interaction), many times acting as a "first impression" for the judge.

In these cases, time is of the essence. Liisa's book provides a road map of a parent's rights and legal recourse. It provides attorneys with a wealth of information and references to case law to promptly (and confidently) take action by filing necessary motions, demanding evidentiary hearings, and making a clean record for appeal. Moreover, it provides judges a reminder as to their responsibilities and obligations in handling custody and parenting time cases in a way that respects both parents' constitutional rights and, more importantly, ensures the children are protected from unnecessary and potentially devastating changes to their lives and relationships with their parents.

It doesn't matter who you are or what your role in a case may be. This book—starting on page one—should be placed on your required reading list.

—ATTORNEY ANDREW BOSSORY, Ann Arbor, MI

Trial court judges have a difficult job. They have heavy caseloads, short time standards to adjudicate cases, little resources to refer families for help, small court budgets, and even smaller staff. By and large judges do an incredible job with difficult cases, horrendous domestic violence, child abuse, many pro se litigants and unprepared attorneys.

As a Family Court judge for twenty years and as a presiding judge of the Family Division for eight years, in the largest court in the State of Michigan, I agree; there are judges who get it wrong. Those judges aren't interested in either keeping abreast of the law, or worse, know the law, but simply don't apply it correctly in their cases. More often than not, however, you get a good judge that had a bad day and got it wrong on the facts or the law or both. In either event, when that happens, this causes immeasurable emotional heartache for a family as well as financial devastation for the parties between paying attorney fees, experts, and appellate fees. It is a tragedy, and we should be vigilant to ensure it doesn't happen to us.

Ms. Speaker is a dedicated appellate attorney, and this book is an excellent resource for litigants, attorneys, referees, and judges alike. Dedicated professionals in family law must stay abreast of the law, present applicable law to the judge, apply the facts of their case to the law, and analyze their case within the proper legal framework. A judge needs to articulate their findings on the record and work through the proper legal analysis. There should always be a record made of anything that is occurring within a courtroom. Attorneys should insist on that to guarantee appellate relief. Lawyers must know and understand the applicable burden of proof and advise their litigants of their chances of success based on that burden. We all must attend regular training and read appellate cases to keep abreast of the law. Know that when you step into a courtroom, you are getting the opinions and lifetime experiences of the judge you are assigned. Empower yourselves with mediation and arbitration whenever possible.

—JUDGE KATHLEEN M. MCCARTHY,
Family Division, Wayne County Circuit Court

Liisa Speaker's compelling and well-written book underscores just how important it is for Family Court judges to "get it right" the first time. While most Family Court judges are sincerely interested in making the best possible decision with the facts in front of them and protecting the best interests of the children and families they serve, they are at times influenced by the outrageous and dramatic behaviors exhibited by parents in family law cases. Occasionally, this can result in reflexive decision making that frequently fails to follow the requirements of the Child Custody Act and the applicable case law. Sadly, these improperly entered orders can take months, even years, to correct. In the meantime, the very children they are charged with protecting suffer disruptive changes of custody that the Child Custody Act specifically seeks to avoid. Ms. Speaker highlights the very real trauma suffered upon these families when this occurs.

—MEDIATOR TRACI RINK, Farmington Hills, MI

Liisa understands the complexity of family law. Family cases should not be determined by how the judge raised her child or a judge's personal opinion, but rather based upon written laws or appellate decisions.

Laws are written to help structure decision making. Family law is codified to protect families, litigants, and children. Before family legislation is codified it is researched, debated, and in most cases is nonpartisan. The structure that laws provide assist the courts in making good decisions in a complex world.

It is imperative that litigants and children have strong advocates and judges who understand that the impact of their decisions can last a lifetime.

This book is a "must read" for Family Court judges, attorneys who practice in Family Court, and appellate judges. Liisa is informative and insightful and will assist trial courts on how to avoid making mistakes that harm families. The Court's goal should be the avoidance of harm.

—HONORABLE SUSAN L. DOBRICH, Family Court Judge since 1995, Chief Judge, Cass County, Michigan

KIDS
CAUGHT
IN  THE
MIDDLE

LIISA SPEAKER

KIDS
CAUGHT
IN  THE
MIDDLE

HOW **FAMILIES ARE HARMED** WHEN
JUDGES DON'T FOLLOW THE LAW

Advantage.

Published by Advantage, Charleston, South Carolina.
Member of Advantage Media Group.

ADVANTAGE is a registered trademark, and the Advantage colophon is a trademark of Advantage Media Group, Inc.

Printed in the United States of America.

10 9 8 7 6 5 4 3 2 1

ISBN: 978-1-64225-296-5
LCCN: 2021919617

Cover design by Megan Elger.
Layout design by Mary Hamilton.

This publication is designed to provide accurate and authoritative information in regard to the subject matter covered. It is sold with the understanding that the publisher is not engaged in rendering legal, accounting, or other professional services. If legal advice or other expert assistance is required, the services of a competent professional person should be sought.

Advantage Media Group is proud to be a part of the Tree Neutral® program. Tree Neutral offsets the number of trees consumed in the production and printing of this book by taking proactive steps such as planting trees in direct proportion to the number of trees used to print books. To learn more about Tree Neutral, please visit **www.treeneutral.com**.

Advantage Media Group is a publisher of business, self-improvement, and professional development books and online learning. We help entrepreneurs, business leaders, and professionals share their Stories, Passion, and Knowledge to help others Learn & Grow. Do you have a manuscript or book idea that you would like us to consider for publishing? Please visit **advantagefamily.com**.

*This book is dedicated to Isadora and Evangeline
and to my family law colleagues who are willing to
step up when the trial judge is not following the law.*

CONTENTS

ACKNOWLEDGMENTS

Over the course of the eighteen months it took me to imagine, plan, and then write this book, I had lots of help along the way.

Thank you to my research assistants who helped me at various stages of the writing process—the fabulous Speaker Law Firm law clerks, both past and current: Ben Pryde, Leonard Peoples Jr., Andrew Malec, Olivia Karujian, and Mariah Ausbury. They were constantly being asked to look up questions about the cases discussed in the book, and surely saved me six months of my time! I am confident that all their research assistance will help you on any bar exam you decide to take.

Thanks to Lisa Schmidt, a fabulous family law attorney and my book editor, for helping me express my vision for the book in a way that will be useful for family law attorneys and approachable for laypeople. Thank you to the team at the Speaker Law Firm, who continued to help our clients, even when I was out of the office for my "writing days." This book should also make it easier for the entire team to better represent our clients. Thanks to the Country Club of Lansing, which graciously allowed me to use their meeting rooms so I could have some quiet space to write my book. And a special thank-you to our clients who allowed us to interview them and share their stories with the world of how trial judges not following the law impacted their children and them as parents.

WHAT IS THIS BOOK ABOUT?

A judge's mistakes can impact a family in many ways. This book shines a light on what happens when judges don't follow the law. It examines the court cases that touch the lives of parents with children—from custody to change of domicile, from grandparenting time to adoption, from guardianship to termination of parental rights. Where are judges making legal mistakes? When are they ignoring the law? What happens after these judges' decisions are appealed and reversed by the higher courts? And most significantly, how are these legal errors impacting our families and our children?

In her dissenting opinion in *O'Brien v D'Annunzio,* Court of Appeals judge Hon. Elizabeth Gleicher confronts the serious problems that arise when trial judges do not follow the law in their initial decision-making, and how those initial errors can follow the family throughout the custody litigation. The overall takeaway from Judge Gleicher's opinion is also the thesis of this book: *When trial judges do not follow the law, it harms children and families.* This book highlights trial judges' legal errors, showing how those bad decisions affect families and children in the long term and even affect how those children view adult relationships and will later raise their own children.

> **When trial judges do not follow the law, it harms children and families.**

The law is the law. It is not acceptable for trial judges to ignore the law when they find it inconvenient or burdensome. Trial judges are the finders of fact in family law cases: they weigh the credibility of witness testimony, they decide whom to believe, and they decide what weight to give documentary evidence. But when it comes to the law, trial judges must follow the steps laid out by the legislature and the higher courts. There should be consequences when trial judges fall short.

WHO SHOULD READ THIS BOOK?

This book is a must-read for family law attorneys. If you occasionally dabble in family law, you need this book even more. It will give you key insights into the problems that are regularly occurring in the trial courts and tips on how to help the trial judge avoid these mistakes in your clients' cases. It also provides areas where we, as attorneys, parents, and judges, need to contribute to see the law further developed. Family law attorneys should raise the issues discussed under "Unresolved Issues" in their trial court cases and develop facts to strengthen that issue on appeal.

If you are a parent who is involved in or anticipates litigation in the family courts, this book will help give insight into what your family law attorney will be facing in court.

If you are a judge who sits on family law cases, you should read this book to avoid the mistakes other judges have made and to be more aware of how judges' decisions impact families and especially children. To be sure, the vast majority of judges in this state are good judges who try to follow the law, yet even good judges make mistakes. But if judges would more consistently follow the law, my job would go away. There would be far fewer appeals in family law cases. For the judges who are reading this book, please take away my job! I will find other appeals to pursue.

WHY DID I WRITE THIS BOOK?

The law is designed to protect families. When judges do not follow the law, it demonstrates a lack of care—not only for the families who are impacted by the decision but also for the people of this state who elect legislators to enact the laws that protect our families. I hope you—as a family law attorney, as a parent, and perhaps even as a judge—care to know how bad decisions are made and how they affect our families and our children. I am an appellate attorney who spends the vast majority of my time appealing decisions of family law judges. I have represented families in each of the areas covered by this book. A good number of the cases that are discussed in this book—and all the sidebars with individual stories—were clients that my law firm represented. My mission, and the mission of the Speaker Law Firm, is to persuade judges to follow the law. I believe that children's lives and custodial environments should not be disrupted on a judge's whim. I believe that children achieve stability, maintain permanency, and develop healthy and secure relationships when judges follow the law. When they do not, when they ignore the statutes that govern their decision-making, when they make decisions based on their feelings and impressions of the parents, then they put children at risk of having their lives unnecessarily disrupted.

Sometimes the children's custodial environments need to be changed for their health, safety, and welfare. But a trial judge should not change custody (or make any of the child-related decisions contained in this book) without going through the steps designed to protect the children under their jurisdiction. Each of the areas covered in this book have statutes that govern how judges make their decisions, often step-by-step. Problems occur when judges decide to not follow the statutes. If judges follow the statute before changing the custodial environment or otherwise making a decision that impacts a child's life, then the chances of the child being harmed by that decision decrease, as do the chances of that decision being reversed on appeal. When judges follow the law, it is more likely that the judge will be doing what is best for the child's health, safety, and welfare. Conversely, when judges don't follow the law, it is less likely the judge will reach the correct result.

A QUICK EXPLANATION OF THE LAYOUT OF THIS BOOK

This book contains twelve chapters, each of which covers some aspect of child-related cases. Although you are invited to do so, *you do not need to read this book from cover to cover.* You can pick and choose chapters that interest you. I do recommend, however, that you read the first chapter—about due process violations—as it sets the stage for legal errors that will be explored in the next eleven chapters.

Each chapter begins by stating the premise of the statute that governs that topic (labeled "Purpose of the Law"). Each chapter then provides a short summary of the law governing this topic. The third section of each chapter dives into problem areas—that is, decisions where trial judges are frequently appealed. Each chapter also covers unresolved areas of law. These are typically topics that do not have a published opinion from the Court of Appeals or the Supreme Court on that issue, and where binding authority is needed. Occasionally, the issue may have been resolved by a published opinion, but I don't agree that the decision follows the law, and I believe the issue should be challenged again. Lastly, each chapter concludes with "Key Takeaways."

This book is not intended to be a legal treatise or law review article, but rather an exploration of where trial judges are going wrong and how bad decisions are impacting families and children. Accordingly, citations to cases and statutes appear in a "Resources" section at the end of each chapter. Finally, there is a glossary at the end of the book. The first time a word or phrase that appears in the glossary is used in each chapter, that word or phrase will be in bold text, identifying it as a defined term—for example: **established custodial environment**.

CHAPTER ONE

DUE PROCESS VIOLATIONS

Parents Fighting for Their Constitutional Rights

THE PURPOSE OF DUE PROCESS

Due process of law is the right to have notice and opportunity to be heard before the government infringes on your right to life, liberty, or property. In family law cases, parents have a liberty interest related to the parenting of their children. Therefore, before infringing on a parent's rights, the courts are required to give parents due process of law.

QUICK LEGAL SUMMARY OF DUE PROCESS IN CHILD-RELATED CASES

The concept of "due process of law" is embedded throughout this book. It derives from the Fifth and Fourteenth Amendments of the United States Constitution. Due process of law is the idea that, before a judge can make a decision affecting a person's rights, that person must be provided with notice and an opportunity to be heard. According to the United States Supreme Court:

> All parties to a dispute have the right to due process of law in order to resolve the dispute, and due process of law requires that the parties be given a hearing before an unbiased and impartial decision maker as part of the resolution process.

A parent has a constitutional liberty interest in the care, custody, and control of their children. But due process also applies to all court proceedings, whether or not constitutional rights are at stake. If an allegation is made or a claim is filed against a person, that person has the right to know about it and be heard on the allegations before a trial judge decides their fate. That means they have the right to come to court and respond to the allegations, to demonstrate that they are false, or to present their own evidence. As you will see throughout this book, there are times when trial judges violate a parent's rights to due process by making decisions based on the allegations from the other parent (or the state, in child welfare cases) without allowing the parent to present their case.

We are seeing a dangerous trend in child custody disputes where courts are obliterating the requirements of the Child Custody Act for a quick resolution. It's very harmful to Michigan families. It has a long-lasting impact and forever changes familial relationships. It runs afoul of the constitutional protections embodied in the Child Custody Act that protects the parent-child relationship and protects the stability that is necessary for children to grow up to be productive adults in society.

—ATTORNEY TRISH HAAS, Grosse Pointe, MI

PROBLEM AREAS WITH DUE PROCESS VIOLATIONS IN CHILD-RELATED CASES

Due process problems will come up throughout this book when judges fail to follow the law. Each chapter contains an example of a due process challenge.

TEMPORARY ORDERS ENTERED WITHOUT FOLLOWING THE LAW

In *O'Brien v D'Annunzio*, a father walked into court with an emergency motion asking the court to give him full physical custody of his children. The court rubber-stamped his request and suspended the mother's parenting time. The trial judge did not hold an evidentiary hearing before making her decision, did not make factual findings on whether there was proper cause or change of circumstances to modify parenting time or custody, did not make findings on the children's established custodial environment, and did not make findings on the best interests of the children. All these steps are required, even for a temporary custody order. Instead, the trial judge made her decision based on the father's unproven allegations. The trial judge did eventually hold a custody trial, but not until fifteen months after the so-called temporary order had disrupted the children's living situation and suspended the mother's parenting time.

The Court of Appeals acknowledged that the trial judge made legal errors but affirmed anyway, calling those errors harmless. Still, the case is most notable for Judge Gleicher's dissenting opinion. Her dissent points out the problem that occurs when the trial judge's impressions of the parties are formed based on a motion and temporary order, without the benefit of an evidentiary hearing. Judge Gleicher saw that the father's claims had soured the trial judge's opinion of the mother, persuading her to suspend parenting time. Judge Gleicher observed that the trial judge's initial impressions about the parties "became a driving force in the deterioration of the parent-child relationship." This problem is amplified when, "without the benefit of a hearing, the trial court unhesitatingly accepted inflammatory ... [and] exaggerated or false allegations set forth in the emergency motion."

The mother went to the Michigan Supreme Court, and the Supreme Court vacated the trial judge's decision and remanded the case to a different judge. Citing its admonishment in *Daly v Ward*, the Supreme Court reminded trial judges that it is "critical ... that trial courts fully comply with MCL 722.27(1)(c) before entering an order that alters a child's established custodial environment" because "[i]n many instances, it is difficult—if not altogether impossible—to effectively remedy [an error] on appeal and to restore the status quo ante ... without causing undue harm to the child." The Supreme Court agreed with Judge Gleicher. The trial judge's errors in handling the case were *not* harmless.

DELAYS BETWEEN AN IMPROPERLY ENTERED TEMPORARY ORDER AND THE FINAL ORDER

Judge Gleicher's dissenting opinion in *O'Brien* also emphasized the harm caused by the lengthy delay (fifteen months) between the temporary order suspending the mother's parenting time and the final decision following the evidentiary hearing:

> That is why *timely* evidentiary hearings play a vital role in evaluating the need for a custodial change ... there is a natural danger that the *first* message received, especially when bombastic or shocking, will retain a disproportionate impact on a judge's ultimate opinion.... [T]aking of the

actual evidence, under oath and subject to cross-examination, is critical before life-changing judgments are rendered.

In *O'Brien*, like in many other custody cases, an ex parte or interim order was in effect for many months. It is not uncommon for orders to remain in place throughout the divorce litigation—which could last twelve to eighteen months or longer in high-conflict cases. These lengthy pretrial delays can change the child's **established custodial environment**. As the parents battle in court, the children are celebrating birthdays, finishing book reports, and having fights with siblings, all in the care of their temporary custodian. In the meantime, the other parent may be losing out on time with their children, making it hard to maintain that same level of connection. The delay is even longer when counting the time for appeals. The erroneous custody order in *O'Brien* was in place for *forty-three months*!

SYSTEMIC DELAYS IN CUSTODY CASES

Why is there so much delay in reaching custody decisions? It is a perplexing situation in Michigan. By statute, custody cases are given priority ahead of other types of cases. The Michigan Supreme Court monitors how many days a custody case is pending. Yet the circuit courts in Michigan typically schedule their custody trials to occur over several months. Unlike a criminal or civil case—where the trial judge will schedule several days in a row to hear evidence and then make a decision—many family court judges' dockets look like this: a half day of trial in March, another half day in April, one full day in June,

> *Why is there so much delay in reaching custody decisions? It is a perplexing situation in Michigan.*

another half day in July, and then after the close of proofs, the trial judge will issue a bench ruling in a separate hearing in September. Some families must wait even longer between hearings.

This practice is shameful. From one scheduled date to the next, trial judges often forget the evidence they heard in the last session or even confuse the case before them with other cases that they have heard in the meantime. It is no wonder—any person would have trouble remembering the details (even with notes) when the custody trial is spread out over such a long period of time.

> [P]robate and circuit courts should be aware of and comply
> with the statutory procedure that exists to insure the orderly
> and efficient resolution of cases involving both guardianship
> and child custody proceedings.... The courts' failure to abide
> by our [case-flow management] time guidelines [with a
> three-year delay] is distressing in this tragic case.

—JUSTICE MAURA CORRIGAN, dissent in *Unthank v Wolfe*.

These delays are even more stunning considering that the Supreme Court has set standards for child custody cases in order to avoid their occurrence. According to the Supreme Court, most custody cases should be completed within one year. Custody cases are supposed to be held within fifty-six days of the request, and once the hearings are complete, the judge is supposed to issue a decision within twenty-eight days. But these time limits are rarely followed.

The Court of Appeals addressed the court rule on delay in *Burmeister v Cole*. The postjudgment litigation in *Burmeister* began when the father sought custody based on the mother's false accusations that he had sexually abused his daughter, that the mother was alienating the child from him, and that the mother was engaging in medical abuse by subjecting the child to "questioning, forensic interviews, and examinations by multiple individuals" about the alleged sexual abuse and putting the child through "invasive medical gynecological exams." The trial judge declined to enter an ex parte order but referred the motion to a **Friend of the Court (FOC)** referee for a hearing. The referee recommended a change of custody. Based on that recommendation, the trial judge entered an order for the mother to have only supervised parenting time because she "presented a risk of harm" to the child. The trial judge then held an evidentiary hearing over a six-month period and waited an additional ten months to issue her decision. Although the Court of Appeals noted the trial judge's twenty-five-month delay did not comply with the court rule, it said the delay was "not fatal." The Court of Appeals invoked a court rule allowing judges to extend the time for a custody decision "for good cause," but did not explain what "good cause" existed to justify the delay. Rather than reversing the trial judge's decision, the Court of Appeals simply added a cautionary footnote:

> We note that on remand, the trial court must comply with the time deadlines set forth in MCR 3.210. There were multiple delays in this case. These delays and procedural missteps needlessly increased the complexity and duration of this case and were not in the best interests of [the child] or either of the parties. On remand, the trial court must adhere to the proper procedural rules and steps that are in place to facilitate the timely resolution of custody disputes.

It seems fairly easy to establish good cause for delaying the case; the parties' stipulation to an adjournment or the need for psychological evaluations have qualified in other cases. Yet even without good cause, there may not be any remedy to the family who suffered the delays. The *Burmeister* Court acknowledged there was "no specific remedy for such a delay" when there was "no evidence that the delay affected the custody determination or affected a substantial right of plaintiff."

IGNORING LEGAL ERRORS ON GROUNDS THAT THE ERRORS WERE HARMLESS

When the Court of Appeals says there is harmless error, it means that the court agrees that the trial judge made mistakes in its decision-making, but the outcome would have been no different if the trial judge correctly applied the law. Judge Gleicher's dissenting opinion in *O'Brien* challenged the use of this doctrine in a custody case.

> I cannot regard the trial court's initial legal error as harmless, as its consequences flowed into its final decision and poisoned the well. Not only were the children removed from Mother's home; before depriving Mother of *any* contact with her children, Mother was prohibited from seeing them except under supervision, a decision which was made before the court heard from any health professionals. The message this arrangement sent, even to a thirteen-year-old, is unmistakable: something is terribly wrong with Mother. And for a thirteen-year-old girl at war with her mother anyway, the trial court's ruling was an invitation to continue and escalate the conflict. As Father readily admitted, in his house there are no rules.

As Judge Gleicher further observed, the trial judge's hostility and animosity toward the mother in *O'Brien* "cannot be turned off like a light switch" once the trial judge finally hears the evidence. To say that a trial judge's failure to follow the law early in a case is harmless because she eventually did follow the law ignores everything that happened to the family in between.

THE COURT OF APPEALS FAILS TO
CORRECT THE TRIAL JUDGE'S ERRORS

The Court of Appeals is an error-correcting court. Its job is to make sure that trial judges follow the law and to make them fix their errors when they don't. Unfortunately, the decision-making at the Court of Appeals appears to be panel driven—some panels of appellate judges will see a clear legal error and reverse; others will not. It is very troubling that some of the judges on the Court of Appeals just rubber-stamp the trial judge's decisions—even when they violate the law. It is even more disturbing when appellate judges call that violation "harmless error."

Case in point—one week after Judge Gleicher's dissenting opinion in *O'Brien*, the Court of Appeals issued another decision about the same trial judge making the same kind of legal errors as it had in *O'Brien*. In *Jacob* v *Jacob*, a different appeals panel (which included Judge Gleicher) found the trial judge's errors were not harmless and instead violated the parent's due process rights. Not only did the *Jacob* panel reverse the trial judge's decision but it gave its opinion immediate effect. The Court of Appeals also held that "due process entitles a party to have an unbiased judge hear and decide a case" and ordered a new judge be appointed to avoid violating the father's due process rights.

When it comes to the law, there should be consistency on the Court of Appeals. Part of the Court of Appeals's job as an error-correcting court is to make sure that trial judges are applying the law consistently from one county to another, from one trial judge to another, and from one case to another. It is not fair to children or their parents that their futures depend on whether the trial judge will correctly apply the law and which appellate judges happen to be assigned the case on appeal.

LITIGATING AGAINST AN
UNREPRESENTED PARENT

Sometimes when one parent is unrepresented, the judge will try to help that parent too much. For instance, in one case, the trial judge was conducting an evidentiary hearing on a change of custody motion. Because the father did not have an attorney, the judge repeatedly objected to the mother's attorney's questions. In another case, the trial judge called a witness to the stand even though the unrepresented parent did not choose to call any witnesses himself. Some trial judges seem to ask the bulk of the questions to help out the unrepresented parent.

This creates a due process concern for the represented parent because the judge is essentially acting as the advocate for the unrepresented parent instead of a neutral decision maker. This is particularly ominous in family law cases where all trials are decided by the judge, not the jury.

CHANGES TO HOW THE COURT
RULES DEFINE A FINAL ORDER

In 2019, the Michigan Supreme Court amended the court rule for custody appeals and drastically restricted a parent's ability to appeal an unfavorable decision by right. The new rule forces parents to appeal parenting- and grandparenting-time orders by application for leave. Under the former rule, a parent had the right to appeal any postjudgment order "affecting custody." The case law that developed under that old court rule talked about the significant right parents had to time with their children and how taking away parenting time, or awarding grandparenting time, eroded the parent's custodial role. The new court rule undercuts those rights, only permitting an appeal by right when the trial judge grants or denies a motion to change custody or domicile. In all other cases, a parent must ask the Court of Appeals for leave to appeal the trial judge's decision.

Most litigants would prefer to have an appeal by right rather than an application for leave. When there is an appeal by right, a panel of three Court of Appeals judges will review the facts and law, allow the parties to present arguments, and issue a written decision explaining why they do or do not agree with the trial judge's decision. On an application for leave to appeal, the party who lost in the trial court must convince the Court of Appeals to take the case. The Court of Appeals only grants approximately 15 percent of all applications. In the 85 percent of cases where the court denies leave, it issues a single-sentence order simply stating: "Denied for lack of merit on the grounds presented." Only if the Court of Appeals grants leave—which means they are persuaded that the trial judge's decision should be reviewed—will the case be given the same treatment as if it had been an appeal by right.

HOW TRIAL JUDGES HANDLE CASES
AFTER BEING REVERSED OR VACATED

This leads us to another recurring problem in family law cases—what happens on remand after the appellate court reverses or vacates the trial judge's decision? Judge Gleicher recommended that the *O'Brien* case be remanded to a different judge, which the Supreme Court eventually did. Now the mother won't need to appear before the same judge who had openly exhibited animosity toward her, resulting in so many legal mistakes, when she returns to the trial court to ask for more parenting time.

The *Jacobs* Court said, "Due process entitles a party to have an unbiased judge hear and decide a case" and ordered a new judge be appointed who would not violate the father's due process rights. In cases where the trial judges' opinions are reversed or vacated, how will the trial judge go about fixing its mistakes? Will they set everyone back to where they were before the mistake was made? Or will trial judges go through the motions and apply the law in ways that keep their original custody decisions in place? There are not any good answers to this problem. What happens on remand varies by judge, how personally invested that judge became in their selected version of the facts, and whether the trial judge is upset that one of the parties challenged their decision on appeal.

THE INTERSECTION OF THE FOC PROCEEDINGS WITH THE TRIAL JUDGE'S DECISION-MAKING

The Michigan Legislature has created the FOC to help lighten the trial judge's workload by investigating issues related to child custody, parenting time, and child support. Every county has a FOC office that is regulated by the Supreme Court (through the FOC Bureau). When directed by a judge, the FOC offices can investigate and make recommendations on custody, parenting time, and child support; offer alternative dispute resolution services; and assist the court in enforcing its child-related orders.

In practice, the FOC's work has two main stages: the investigation or conciliation stage and the referee-hearing stage. Circuit courts across the state have employed a less formal conciliation or investigative process using nonattorney staff called investigators. These investigators will try to find the bridge between the two parents' positions, and if found, can help the parents draft an order to be submitted to the trial judge. Sometimes the investigator will have conversations with the parties and other witnesses, but those conversations are not recorded, and the investigator can consider evidence that would otherwise be inadmissible in a court proceeding (such as police reports, CPS reports, or statements by one parent about what the other parent or child said). If parties cannot reach an agreement, the investigator can make a recommendation on custody and parenting time, which often includes detailed facts about the investigation. The parties can object to the recommendation, and the case will proceed to an evidentiary hearing before the referee or the trial judge. But if neither party objects, the investigator's recommendation becomes the order of the court without a judge ever reviewing it.

Until recently, this informal process was not authorized or regulated by statute. In 2019, the Supreme Court changed the court rules to permit an investigative process in the FOC—now known as the Facilitative Information Gathering Conference (or FIGC). Like the prior informal process, the investigator tries to help the parties reach an agreement, and if the parties do not agree, the FIGC investigator can make a recommendation on parenting time and custody to the court. That recommendation could become the order of the court even while an objection is pending, which raises the same due process concerns as the previous process. But one big difference is that now a party can object to the case being submitted to the FIGC investigator.

An FOC referee—an attorney who is well versed in family law—holds evidentiary hearings. Those hearings are recorded just like a judicial proceeding, and the parties are represented by attorneys who present witnesses and evidence. Like a judicial hearing, the rules of evidence apply (so for example, a CPS report is not admissible, but instead a parent would have to bring in the CPS caseworker who wrote the report to testify about its content). After hearing the evidence, the referee writes an opinion that includes findings of fact under the Child Custody Act—including the established custodial environment and the best-interest factors—and makes a recommendation as to custody and parenting time based on those findings. If the parties do not object, the referee's recommendation will become the order of the court, and the trial judge will have one less case to hear. If either party objects to the referee's decision, then they can request a **de novo hearing** before the trial judge. The judge can choose whether to review **the record** presented to the referee, allow the parties to present their entire case again in court, or some combination of the two.

ALLOWING THE FOC INVESTIGATOR TO TESTIFY AS A WITNESS

In *Roat v Roat,* the mother moved to Colorado before the divorce. The children went back and forth between the two homes several times based on the parties' custody agreement (including after the mother later moved to Nebraska). Eventually the father filed a motion to change custody to keep the children in Michigan. At the custody trial, the father called as a witness the FOC investigator who had met with the parties and made recommendations during the divorce proceedings. She had not met with the parties during the postjudgment custody litigation. Although all witnesses were supposed to be **sequestered**, the FOC investigator had apparently been in the courtroom for part of the trial and offered her opinion based on her prior knowledge of the case. After hearing all the testimony, including that of the FOC investigator, the trial judge made fact-findings and awarded physical custody to the father.

However, the trial judge did not decide the issues of legal custody or the mother's parenting time. Instead he referred those two issues to the FOC. The very next day, that same FOC investigator issued her recommendation, relying on the trial judge's best-interest findings from the custody trial. The trial judge adopted the investigator's recommendation the same day. The Court of Appeals agreed with the mother that the trial judge erred by adopting the investigator's recommendation entered without an opportunity for the FOC to hear evidence on legal custody and parenting time and without giving the mother an opportunity to object to her recommendation. The Court of Appeals vacated the legal custody and parenting-time rulings and remanded the case so the trial judge could hear the mother's objections. The Court of Appeals, however, did not address the mother's constitutional challenge as to the violation of due process.

PREVENTING A PARENT FROM OBJECTING TO THE FRIEND OF COURT RECOMMENDATION

In *Gable v Merrill*, the mother had been the children's primary caretaker for their entire lives. She moved seventy miles away and wanted to change the children's school, but the father would not consider it. Instead he marched to the courthouse the minute he got off the phone with her and filed a motion to change custody. On the date of the referee hearing, the mother—who did not have an attorney—mistook the time of the hearing, believing that it started thirty minutes later than it actually did. The referee took the father's testimony, and one minute after the father finished his testimony, the mother entered the courtroom. However, because the referee had already begun giving his ruling seconds before, he refused to allow the mother the opportunity to present any evidence. The referee recommended that the father be awarded custody, and the mother filed an objection and a request for a de novo hearing before the trial judge. Yet the trial judge refused to allow the mother to present any evidence at the de novo hearing due to her late arrival at the referee hearing. The judge ultimately upheld the bulk of the referee's decision, drastically changing the children's physical custody and flipping the parenting-time arrangement without ever hearing any testimony or other evidence from the mother, the children's lifelong primary caregiver.

The mother argued on appeal that the court's procedures violated her due process rights. Even though the FOC Act allows the trial judge to "impose reasonable restrictions" during the de novo hearing, those restrictions are only allowed when "[t]he parties have been given a full opportunity to present and preserve important evidence at the referee hearing." It also requires the trial judge to afford the parties "a new opportunity to offer the same evidence to the court as was presented to the referee and to supplement that evidence with evidence that could not have been presented to the referee."

The Court of Appeals agreed with the mother that the trial judge should have allowed her to present evidence at the de novo hearing. The Court of Appeals recognized that the purpose of both the FOC Act and the Child Custody Act is to protect and promote the best interests of the children. The Court of Appeals suggested that the trial judge could have sanctioned the mother for showing up late to the FOC hearing, but it was clear legal error to change the custody of the children without allowing the mother to present evidence in their best interests: "[T]he children's best interests necessitated the trial court hearing both sides in determining whether to change a custody arrangement in which the children had spent a large portion of their lives." The Court of Appeals retained jurisdiction so it could keep a watchful eye on what the trial judge did next. On remand, the trial judge awarded custody to the mother and set up a parenting-time schedule for the father.

PRACTICE TIP: *Preservation of an issue is essential to protecting the clients' interests on appeal. When a trial judge refuses to hold a hearing, preservation becomes difficult. Trial attorneys should file an objection to the FOC recommendation or file a motion for relief from judgment raising the due process violation to ensure the issue is part of the record before the appeal is filed.*

TRIAL JUDGE'S UNCLEAR APPOINTMENT OF AN L-GAL OR GAL

A repeated problem in family law cases occurs when a judge appoints a **Lawyer Guardian Ad Litem (L-GAL)** or a **Guardian Ad Litem (GAL)** but does not clearly delineate which one. Even though the names sound similar, the two roles are very different. An L-GAL is an attorney who is appointed to advocate for the child—the child's attorney in the custody case. As an attorney, the L-GAL can examine witnesses and otherwise advocate for what is in the child's best interests. In contrast, a GAL is appointed to advise the trial judge. The GAL does not have to be an attorney but often is. The GAL can make a recommendation to the trial judge about what the GAL believes is in the child's best interest and can be asked to testify in court about that recommendation, though they call no witnesses themselves. When the parties to the case—and the attorneys representing them—do not know the role the attorney is filling, there is a risk that the trial judge will violate due process by allowing or prohibiting the L-GAL or GAL to act in a way that is contrary

Preservation of an issue is essential to protecting the clients' interests on appeal.

to the appointment, hampering the parents' abilities to present their custody case.

In *Strech v Bush*, both parents filed motions to modify parenting time. Because the litigation had been contentious, the trial judge appointed an attorney to serve as the GAL. The appointed attorney investigated the case, talked to the parents, wrote a report on the child's best interest, and recommended that parenting time remain the same. At trial, the father wanted to call the GAL as a witness, but the trial judge denied the request, ruling that she was actually an L-GAL. The Court of Appeals held that the trial judge interfered with the parent's right to examine the GAL and to controvert her report. "While [the GAL] is an attorney by trade, she was not serving as an attorney or an L-GAL in this case. [The GAL] created a report to help the court assess [the child's] best interests, and allowing the parties to examine the author on the stand furthers that interest." The Court of Appeals remanded the case to the trial judge to continue the evidentiary hearing so that the parties could call the GAL to the stand as a witness.

For parents going through custody litigation, they have the right to know which specific role, GAL or L-GAL, the judge is appointing this third party who holds such a critical role in the litigation. Even more importantly, once the court assigns the specific role, the appointed person must not conflate or confuse the duties and responsibilities of that specific role. It would be like a person showing up to play in their recreational softball-league championship game only to find out that the game's umpire was going to play dual roles as both the umpire and the coach of the opposing team at the same time. Certain roles cannot be combined without completely destroying the fairness of the process.

—**JOHN KLINE**, attorney, Ann Arbor, MI

UNRESOLVED ISSUES ON THE DUE PROCESS FRONT

From working on hundreds of cases and reviewing thousands more, there are virtually endless possibilities for how trial judges can violate a parent's due process rights. It seems that the creative ways in which a judge might avoid following the law are limited only by the imaginations of the attorneys and judge on the case. This is not to say that the judges or attorneys recognize that they are violating due process. But those violations do frequently occur, whether intended or not.

The Friend of the Court (FOC) is a key constituent among those of us who have chosen to spend our lives trying to help resolve families' legal problems. Given the resounding influence of the FOC on the futures of so many people, most importantly children, we cannot offer the FOC enough support in all realms, from training to staffing. Compassionate, well-educated help from the FOC is irreplaceable. Unlike having a private mediator whom the parties agree upon, the FOC staff person assigned to the case is not typically chosen by the parties. This introduces an element of the unknown that attorneys do not usually welcome. Results can vary widely depending upon which referee or investigator is assigned to the case.

—**LORI BUITEWEG**, attorney, Ann Arbor, MI

FOC INVESTIGATIONS AND CONCILIATIONS

Family law attorneys have concerns that some FOC offices around the state—particularly their investigators or caseworkers—have processes that deprive parents of due process. For example:

- Many times, when one parent files a parenting-time complaint with the FOC, that complaint is not served on the other parent (or their attorney). The complaints start piling up without the other parent ever knowing they have been filed or having an opportunity to respond, explain what happened, or even refute that parenting time was denied.

- The investigator will question one parent about the contents of documents obtained from the other parent without showing them the documents. This denies the responding parent an opportunity to defend themselves or produce other evidence to contradict the documents the investigator is relying on.

- The investigators will use the child interview to find out the "truth" about what is happening in each parent's home rather than limiting it to the child's reasonable preference.

JENNIFER'S STORY:

Mother Loses Custody after Noninjury Accident

Jennifer had been the primary caretaker of her son for his entire seven years of life. One day, while Jennifer was at work, her boyfriend drove with her son in the car after consuming alcohol. He had an accident. Thankfully no one was injured, but it prompted the boy's father to request custody.

An FOC investigator recommended a custody change, and the trial judge rubber-stamped the investigator's decision. It made Jennifer feel that the judge would not listen to her side of the story as the mother. Her son was shocked and very upset when he was taken away from his mother's home. He had looked forward to coming back home. But after the

Court of Appeals overturned the judge's decision, it went back to the same judge—he did not change his mind.

"The trial judge never wanted to listen to anything I had to say and was only interested in what the father was saying."

ADOPTING AN INVESTIGATOR'S FINDINGS WITHOUT AN EVIDENTIARY HEARING

There are many cases that address the problem of a trial judge adopting the FOC investigator's findings and recommendation. As discussed above, the investigator's role is significantly different than that served by the referee. A referee or trial judge should not rely on the investigator's findings because the investigative process is less formal than a judicial proceeding. When a referee or judge relies on the investigator's fact-findings, they are likely considering facts presented to the investigator without the benefit of an attorney and without regard to the rules of evidence. Considering the investigator's findings presents a due process violation for the parent, who has the right to have their motion decided by a jurist based on the rules of evidence.

In *Bowling v McCarrick* (see "Jennifer's Story"), the father filed a motion to change custody, and the parties individually met with an FOC investigator. Based on private interviews and other documents, the investigator issued findings and recommended that the father have custody. The mother objected. The trial judge held a short hearing and upheld the investigator's recommendation. The mother challenged the violation of due process when the trial judge relied on the investigator's findings, which were contained in a lengthy report. The Court of Appeals did not address how a trial judge violates a parent's due process rights by relying on the investigator's findings to reach its custody decision. Instead, the court held that the trial judge erred by allowing the investigator to make the threshold decision of proper cause or change of circumstances.

This scenario poses a great problem because so many circuit courts around this state refer cases to an investigator to save court resources. When a parent objects to the investigator's recommendation, the parties should be permitted to present their evidence anew before the referee or the trial judge. The investigative arm of the FOC is supposed to help parents resolve their disputes more quickly, without the need for a hearing before the trial judge. By allowing investigator recommendations to become an order of the court, it transforms an invitation to settle the case into a demand to settle—or else the investigator's findings will become the order of the court.

The Child Custody Act imposes on the trial court a duty to ensure that the resolution of any custody dispute is in the best interests of the children ... No statute or court rule provides any circumstances under which a trial court may be excused from this legislatively mandated duty when the Friend of the Court, upon order of the court, has conducted an investigation and provided a report and recommendation.

—HON. JANE E. MARKEY, *Wlodyka v Wlodyka*

DELEGATING JUDICIAL AUTHORITY TO A GAL (WHO MAY NOT EVEN BE AN ATTORNEY)

A similar problem occurs when the trial judge delegates too much authority to a GAL. As noted above, the role of the GAL is to assist the judge in figuring out the children's best interest. But what if the judge accepts the GAL's recommendation without a hearing, presentation of evidence, or any independent fact-finding? This would result in a violation of the parent's due process rights because it permits a person to decide the parent's custody and parenting time—often based on hearsay or otherwise inadmissible evidence—with no opportunity for the parent to make a case to the judge that the GAL's recommendation was incorrect. Some trial judges have even allowed a GAL to make binding recommendations that take interim effect (pending an objection and hearing before the trial judge). The Court of Appeals has reversed trial judges' orders granting a Friend of Court investigator that authority, so delegating it to a GAL should be no different. The Court of Appeals has been inconsistent in its rulings on this point, likely because its decisions have all been unpublished. In at least one case, *Deling v Lam*, the Court of Appeals identified the trial judge's improper delegation to the GAL when it simply adopted the GAL's report and findings on custody. Similarly in *Underhill v Underhill*, the trial judge was not permitted to allow the child's therapist to make parenting-time decisions.

KEY TAKEAWAYS

- Courts are required to grant <u>due process of law</u> to protect parents' liberty interests in the <u>care, custody, and control</u> of their children, as well as <u>notice</u> and an <u>opportunity to be heard.</u>

- Even for <u>temporary custody orders,</u> the court must make factual findings to support its decision.

- Despite mandates <u>prioritizing custody cases,</u> trial courts continually schedule custody hearings over the span of many months.

- FOC has two main stages: (1) the <u>investigation stage</u> with nonattorney staff to reach a settlement; and (2) the <u>referee stage</u> with a family law attorney who holds evidentiary hearings and makes a recommendation.

- A Lawyer Guardian Ad Litem acts as the child's attorney, whereas the Guardian Ad Litem provides a recommendation to the judge regarding the child's best interest.

RESOURCES FOR CHAPTER ONE

DUE PROCESS

Daly v Ward, 501 Mich 897; 901 NW2d 897 (2017).

Mathews v Eldridge, 424 US 319; 96 S Ct 893;47 L Ed 2d 18 (1976).

Tumey v Ohio, 273 US 510; 47 S Ct 437; 71 L Ed 749 (1927).

Withrow v Larkin, 421 US 35; 95 S Ct 1456; 43 L Ed 2d 712 (1975).

Jacob v Jacob, unpublished per curiam opinion of Court of Appeals, issued March 3, 2020 (Docket Nos. 344580, 344598, 344654, 344809, 344894, 347014, and 350162).

O'Brien v D'Annunzio, unpublished per curiam opinion of Court of Appeals, issued February 27, 2020 (Docket No. 347830), rev'd by __ Mich ___ (2021).

Wlodyka v Wlodyka, unpublished per curiam opinion of Court of Appeals, issued March 15, 2021 (Docket No. 356214).

Michigan Judicial Institute, *Judicial Disqualification in Michigan* (2021), p. 1, <https://mjieducation.mi.gov/documents/benchbooks/25-jdq> (accessed June 11, 2021).

PARENTING-TIME DECISIONS

Roat v Roat, unpublished per curiam opinion of the Court of Appeals, issued March 17, 2020 (Docket No. 350299).

Underhill v Underhill, unpublished per curiam opinion of the Court of Appeals, issued November 1, 2016 (Docket No. 331897).

DECISION DELAYS

Unthank v Wolfe, 483 Mich 964; 763 NW2d 924 (2009).
MCR 3.210(C)(7).

FRIEND OF THE COURT

Bowling v McCarrick, 318 Mich App 568; 899 NW2d 808 (2016).

State Court Administrative Office, *Michigan Friend of The Court: A Guide to Custody, Parenting Time and Support* <https://www.legislature.mi.gov/Publications/Friend_of_the_Court-WEB.pdf> (accessed June 10, 2021).

MCL 552.505.

MCR 3.224.

MCL 552.503.

MCL 552.507.

GALS AND L-GALS

Deling v Lam, unpublished per curiam opinion of the Court of Appeals, issued October 7, 2010 (Docket No. 295272).

Strech v Bush, unpublished per curiam opinion of the Court of Appeals, issued September 10, 2020 (Docket No. 351196).

MCL 722.24.

MCL 712A.17d.

DE NOVO HEARINGS

Gable v Merrill, unpublished per curiam opinion of Court of Appeals, issued September 19, 2019 (Docket No. 347814).

MCR 3.215.

CHAPTER TWO

CHILD CUSTODY

*When the Initial Custody
Proceeding Goes Wrong*

●　　　●　　　●

THE PURPOSE OF CHILD CUSTODY LAW

To avoid disruptions of the child's **established custodial environment** unless there is a very compelling reason.

QUICK LEGAL SUMMARY OF INITIAL CHILD CUSTODY DECISIONS

When trial judges are making initial custody decisions, such as in a judgment of divorce or child custody order, there are several steps they must take. Typically, there is some sort of **temporary order** or **interim order** in place, often resulting from the **Friend of the Court (FOC)** process. Even so, the trial judge still must make findings to support their decision in the custody judgment or judgment of divorce. To do that properly, the trial judge must first determine who has the established custodial environment with the children. Oftentimes with divorcing parents, the children will naturally look to both parents because, leading up to the divorce, both parents were living in the same house as the children. However, as the case drags on and the children spend more time with one parent, the established custodial environment may shift toward that parent and away from the other.

After deciding which parent or parents have an established custodial environment with the children, the trial judge will then know which **burden of proof** to apply. **Clear and convincing evidence** is appropriate if the trial judge's decision changes the established custodial environment from one parent to the other or from both parents to one. The only time the trial judge can apply the lower **preponderance of the evidence** standard in an initial custody determination is when neither parent has an established custodial environment with the children (which is very rare), or when both parents share an established custodial environment and the trial judge awards joint physical custody (which is very common).

The trial judge then applies the appropriate burden of proof to the best-interest factors under the Child Custody Act. These factors are the driving force for every child custody decision in this state. They are:

a. The love, affection, and other emotional ties existing between the parties involved and the child.

b. The capacity and disposition of the parties involved to give the child love, affection, and guidance and to continue the education and raising of the child in his or her religion or creed, if any.

c. The capacity and disposition of the parties involved to provide the child with food, clothing, medical care or other remedial care, and other material needs.

d. The length of time the child has lived in a stable, satisfactory environment, and the desirability of maintaining continuity.

e. The permanence, as a family unit, of the existing or proposed custodial home or homes.

f. The moral fitness of the parties involved.

g. The mental and physical health of the parties involved.

h. The home, school, and community record of the child.

i. The reasonable preference of the child, if the court considers the child to be of sufficient age to express preference.

j. The willingness and ability of each of the parties to facilitate and encourage a close and continuing parent-child relationship between the child and the other parent or the child and the parents.

k. Domestic violence, regardless of whether the violence was directed against or witnessed by the child.

l. Any other factor considered by the court to be relevant to a particular child custody dispute.

The best-interest analysis is not a mathematical calculation. The trial judge looks to the "sum total" of those factors and can give more or less weight to certain factors based on the evidence. Once they complete their best-interest analysis, the trial judge can make a custody ruling.

The best-interest analysis is not a mathematical calculation.

A judge who fails to follow the requirements of the Child Custody Act creates further acrimony between the litigants, which in turn harms the very children whom the statutes aim to protect.

—**ANDREW COHEN,** attorney, Southfield, MI

PROBLEM AREAS IN INITIAL CHILD CUSTODY DECISIONS

LACK OF FINDINGS ON THE ESTABLISHED CUSTODIAL ENVIRONMENT

It is shocking how many times trial judges fail to determine which parent or parents have established custodial environments with the children before deciding custody disputes. According to the Child Custody Act, the established custodial environment is defined as which parent the child looks to for "guidance, discipline, the necessities of life, and parental comfort" over an "appreciable time." Without making a finding on the established custodial environment, the appellate courts will never know if the trial judge's best-interest analysis was appropriate in the first place. Failure to make a finding on the established custodial environment also directly contravenes the purpose of the Child Custody Act—to avoid unnecessary disruptions in the child's life.

In *Kessler v Kessler*, the Court of Appeals reversed the trial judge's order that failed to make findings on the established custodial environment. The family lived in Muskegon County, but during the divorce proceedings, the mother obtained a job in Florida and wanted the children to move there with her. The trial judge did not determine the children's established custodial environment because it did not believe it was necessary, since the parties were living together in the marital home up until the custody trial. The trial judge then awarded custody to the father using a preponderance of the evidence standard. The Court of Appeals reversed, holding that the "failure to determine whether there is an established custodial environment is not harmless error because the trial court's determination regarding whether an established custodial environment exists determines the proper burden of proof in regard to the best interests of the children." On remand, the trial judge had to first decide whether the established custodial environment was with the mother, father, or both parents before addressing custody.

When a trial judge makes this type of mistake, the appellate courts should be willing to reverse immediately without waiting for a full briefing or oral argument. A failure to make a finding on the established custodial environment will more often than not result in a reversal by the appellate courts and remand to the trial judge. But many judges on the Court of Appeals are reluctant to grant **peremptory reversal** (as a matter of principle or policy), even when it is clear that the issue should be taken care of right away. This means more delay for the family. Even when a trial judge's decision is eventually reversed, the time it takes to obtain that appellate reversal means that families and children are living under the trial judge's new (and possibly erroneous) custody arrangement for months while the appeal is pending.

WHEN CHILDREN DO NOT HAVE AN ESTABLISHED CUSTODIAL ENVIRONMENT WITH EITHER PARENT

In *Bowers v Bowers*, the parties lived together in New Jersey while the father was stationed there for military service. By agreement, the son went with his father to California on reassignment, and the daughter stayed with her mother in New Jersey. Then the father sent his son from California to Michigan to live with the paternal grandparents. When the father completed his military service, he joined them in Michigan. The mother and daughter moved to Michigan later that year. Initially, the custody arrangement was for the children to spend every weekend together, alternating between parents. The father filed for divorce and was awarded custody of both children. Ultimately, the trial judge found that the children had an established custodial environment with both parents, but the Court of Appeals disagreed. Instead the court held that the children's frequent moves and the parties' extensive ongoing custody litigation (which resulted in two appeals and two reversals) left them with "no expectation of permanency" as to whom they looked to for guidance, discipline, necessities of life, and comfort.

BEST-INTEREST FACTORS

Another frequent area of appeal in custody cases is when the trial judge does not go through each of the twelve best-interest factors, weighing whether each factor favors the mother, the father, neither parent, or both parents. This problem has lessened in recent years, but only after many appellate decisions have called for a careful review of each and every factor.

BROOKE'S STORY:
Lengthy Trial Did Not Justify Judge's Favoring Father

Brooke and her husband had a volatile relationship. Brooke was the primary caretaker for their two-year-old son and newborn daughter. The father's parenting time was limited, particularly early in the case because their infant daughter was still nursing. The divorce litigation was contentious and lasted over two and a half years. The father's testimony took up approximately half of the twenty-three-day trial, including descriptions of how he had deputized his young son into the "truth police" to help the child with his interactions with his mother and grandmother.

The trial judge's decision was based primarily on the parents' strained relationship and his belief that Brooke would not adequately facilitate a relationship between the children and their father. The trial judge failed to consider that the father degraded Brooke in front of the children and was no more likely to facilitate her relationship with the children.

The trial judge found that the children's established custodial environment was with their mother but granted the father sole physical and legal custody, only granting Brooke parenting time on alternating weekends and four hours midweek.

Although the court of appeals reversed the judge's custody decision as against the great weight of the evidence, the trial judge on remand refused to consider up-to-date information, including evidence about problems in the father's home. Using only the evidence from trial, the judge kept his original decision in place. The court of appeals reversed again.

The young children did not understand why they were suddenly living full time with their father. Brooke's son yelled at her and thought she did not love him anymore. Her young daughter had never even spent two consecutive nights with her father when the judge changed custody. The father has used his victory in the trial court to wield even more power. Sadly, because the father violated the court's orders without any consequence, Brooke ultimately settled for one extra overnight per week, feeling the trial judge would never rule in her favor.

It can be even more difficult to appeal errors in the trial judge's best-interest findings. Appellate courts give deference to trial judges' factual findings; they will not second-guess what a trial judge finds as long as it is supported by the evidence. To reverse the trial judge's findings, the appellate court must conclude that the findings were **clearly erroneous** or that the overall best-interest analysis is **against the great weight of the evidence**.

Although it is very difficult to prevail in an appeal challenging the trial judge's best-interest findings, it is not impossible. In *Holmes v Holmes* (see "Brooke's Story"), the trial judge found that the mother, who had been the primary caretaker of the children during the marriage and the divorce proceedings, should not have custody and instead awarded sole legal and sole physical custody to the father. The Court of Appeals reversed the trial judge's best-interest findings because they were against the great weight of the evidence. Specifically, the Court of Appeals disagreed with the trial judge's analysis on three best-interest factors, which the trial judge weighed in favor of the father, finding those factors should have been neutral.

The trial judge weighed factor (b) in the father's favor—the capacity and disposition of the parties involved to give the children love, affection, and guidance. In finding for the father, the trial judge relied on:

- the mother's reducing the parties' wedding guest list;

- not allowing her mother-in-law's dog in her Montana home;

- supervising the father's parenting time with the three-year-old;

- not involving the father in the infant's birth;

- changing the father's parenting time with the infant to supervised when he was late returning the infant; and

- not involving the father in decisions related to daycare and preschool.

These facts did not pertain at all to factor (b). If relevant at all, they pertained to factor (j)—the willingness of the parties to facilitate a parent-child relationship. The trial judge failed to consider the mother's bond with the children.

As for the moral fitness factor (f), the trial judge also wrongly weighed that factor in favor of the father. The trial judge relied on the fact that the mother stole a wedding picture from the father's sister, and that the father established the "truth police" with the three-year-old "[i]n part because [the mother] controlled the child." Moral fitness pertains to a parent's conduct that has a "significant influence on how one will function as a parent." The father established the truth police after there were unsubstantiated abuse allegations against him.

However, the mother denied reporting him to CPS. The trial judge also failed to consider how the truth police itself weighed against the father's own moral fitness as a parent. The Court of Appeals instructed the trial judge to reexamine its best-interest findings—ordering the trial judge "to review the entire question of custody" and consider again "all the statutory factors."

> **PRACTICE TIP:** *When appealing a trial judge's factual findings, it is important that the appellate court has access to the entire record, including trial exhibits. Many trial courts do not retain the admitted exhibits after a final order is entered. Trial attorneys should preserve both parties' trial binders and make notes about what exhibits were admitted or rejected to ensure the record is complete on appeal.*

TRIAL JUDGE'S OBLIGATION TO CONSIDER UP-TO-DATE EVIDENCE ON REMAND

According to the Michigan Supreme Court's decision in *Fletcher v Fletcher*, after an appellate court reverses a case, the trial judge must "consider up-to-date information, including the children's reasonable preferences, as well as the fact that the children have been living with the other parent during the appeal and any other changes in circumstances arising since the trial court's original custody order." Unfortunately, not all trial judges honor this directive, and the Court of Appeals has not been consistent in directing trial judges' actions following remand in a custody case.

There are many cases where the Court of Appeals instructs the lower court to consider up-to-date evidence. For example, in *Kessler v Kessler* (discussed above), the Court of Appeals instructed the trial judge to "consider up-to-date information and any other changes in circumstances arising since the trial court's original custody order." In *Pierron v Pierron*—a school-change case that resulted in a change of custody—the Court of Appeals stated that on remand, the trial judge "should consider up-to-date information including, but not limited to, the current and reasonable preferences of the minor children and any other changes that may have arisen in the interim period."

Trial judges must still abide by *Fletcher*, even when the Court of Appeals does not mention its requirements. In the *Holmes* case (discussed above), the trial judge refused to consider up-to-date evidence and instead only considered the evidence presented during the divorce trial twenty-two months earlier. The trial judge redid its custody decision to address the problems identified by the Court of Appeals and came to the same conclusion. As a result, the mother was forced to file another appeal on the custody decision, along with a motion for peremptory reversal. The Court of Appeals granted her peremptory request because the trial judge failed to follow the mandates of *Fletcher*.

MICHAEL'S STORY:
The Judge Enters a Temporary Order Allowing the Children to Move Seven Hours Away

Michael and his wife had been married for fourteen years and were the proud parents of three boys—ages nine, five, and four. The family lived in the western Upper Peninsula, where the boys enjoyed many outdoor activities. When the mom filed for divorce, she obtained a temporary order from the judge that allowed her to move the boys seven hours away from the home and community they had known their entire lives without following the law on established custodial environment or best interests.

Michael filed an emergency appeal, and the court of appeals reversed right away, but then the trial judge disregarded the court's instructions, and Michael had to file an emergency motion in the appeal. Again, the court of appeals sided with Michael.

With the abrupt changes imposed by the judge's temporary orders, the boys were "super confused about their new school, what town they lived in, who they were living with." They had to go to counseling a couple of times a week, fell behind on homework, didn't receive report cards due to multiple moves, and missed out on hockey, their Christmas concert, and First Communion. The youngest child started showing signs of separation anxiety, begging to sleep with his dad and go to work with him. The middle son started sucking his thumb again. The judge's bad rulings had an "emotional and mental toll on the children."

Eventually, the judge allowed the boys to stay with their father during the week but spend every weekend with their mother— which required a seven- to eight-hour drive each way.

EX PARTE OR TEMPORARY ORDERS

Trial judges often enter interim or ex parte orders early in the case without making the appropriate fact-findings. Many times, that interim or temporary custody order is in place for a very long time. That can create an established custodial environment for the children with one parent or the other. One solution is to appeal the temporary order sooner and more frequently rather than waiting for the final custody decision before filing an appeal.

When an ex parte or interim order grants custody to one parent and limits the other parent's time, that initial decision sets the stage for the trial judge's ultimate decision. When an ex parte or interim order is entered without the requisite best-interest findings, there is no assurance that it is in the child's best interest. That faulty decision could lay the groundwork to continue the faulty custody arrangement in the final order. The trial judge will not want to disrupt the established custodial environment created by the faulty interim or ex parte order.

The problem is not just that the ex parte or temporary order is in place for a long time. Those orders are frequently based solely on one parent's untested allegations about the other parent. Trial judges do not typically hold evidentiary hearings—even though they are supposed to hold at least an abbreviated one—before issuing temporary custody orders. For example, in one case (see "Michael's Story"), as soon as the mother filed for divorce, she asked the trial judge to award her custody so that she could move with her children from the western Upper Peninsula of Michigan to Gaylord—seven hours away—even though she did not have family or friends anywhere near Gaylord. The trial judge granted her request, uprooting the children's lives, without making any findings or hearing any evidence on the children's established custodial environment or their best interests. The father appealed, and the Court of Appeals reversed because it was imperative that the trial judge make those fact-findings before allowing the children's custodial environment to shift to the mother in another part of the state. At the next hearing, the trial judge was incredulous that she had been reversed. She insisted that the children could still move to Gaylord before the parties presented evidence. Another motion before the Court of Appeals remedied that situation, and eventually the trial judge made her findings that both parents had the established custodial environment. Thankfully the parties settled after that, allowing the children to remain in the family home where they had grown up, attend their original schools, and generally enjoy the lifestyle they had always experienced.

> **PRACTICE TIP:** *Trial attorneys should be alert to legal errors made in temporary custody orders early in the case and consider filing appeals with motions for peremptory reversal. Waiting to appeal a final order can leave your clients waiting months, or even years, to correct a clear error. By that time, the established custodial environment may have changed, further reducing their chances before the trial judge.*

TRIAL JUDGES RUBBER-STAMPING INITIAL ORDERS FROM THE FRIEND OF COURT

It is common in many counties across Michigan to have the FOC make an initial custody decision—on a temporary basis—while the case proceeds through the court system. Depending on each county's FOC office, that initial decision might come from a nonattorney investigator (discussed in chapter 1) or an attorney referee. The investigator will often interview the parents (without their

Waiting to appeal a final order can leave your clients waiting months, or even years, to correct a clear error.

attorneys) and then make a recommendation for temporary custody. In contrast, the referee uses a more formal process, which includes an evidentiary hearing with the assistance of the parents' attorneys. In both scenarios, the FOC employee will write an opinion stating the facts, go through a best-interest analysis, and make a temporary custody recommendation, which very often becomes the order of the trial court, at least on a temporary basis. Through this process, an established custodial environment might be created while waiting for the trial judge to make its final custody decision.

Although the FOC investigator or referee usually makes fact-findings to support their recommendation, that is not always true. *Grooms v Huntzinger* involved two unmarried parents of a newborn child who could not agree on a custody arrangement. The investigator recommended a phased parenting-time plan, which ramped up to three consecutive overnights before the child was six months old, while the infant was still nursing. The trial judge adopted the investigator's recommendation, even though it was contrary to the parenting-time statute for children under one year of age, the Michigan Parenting Time Guideline for children under four years of age, and the recommendation of the child's pediatrician. The trial judge adopted the investigator's recommendation in a temporary order without hearing any evidence or conducting any analysis of the best-interest factors. Although the Court of Appeals denied the mother's emergency application for leave to appeal, the Supreme Court reversed and remanded to the Court of Appeals for consideration as on leave granted. Following this ruling, the parties settled.

FIXING LEGAL ERRORS QUICKLY—OR NOT

When trial judges make legal errors in child custody cases, the Court of Appeals should **peremptorily reverse** the decision so the trial judge can correct the error quickly. Recognizing that many appellate judges are reluctant to peremptorily reverse, Judge Peter O'Connell's dissenting opinion in *Marik v Marik* recommended that the Supreme Court adopt a court rule of "inevitable remand." If a case would inevitably have to be remanded due to a trial judge's failure to make findings, then the Court of Appeals should remand it at the outset of the appeal rather than waiting for a full decision on the merits.

> [W]hen the trial transcript is devoid of a trial court's findings on which party has, or which parties share, the established custodial environment, a motion to remand should immediately be filed with the Court of Appeals. The motion should articulate that the trial court erred and request a remand for an evidentiary hearing for the trial court to decide which party has, or which parties share, the [established custodial environment].

While Judge O'Connell's dissent in *Marik* referred to a failure to make findings on the established custodial environment, the same principle applies to other legal errors by the trial judge, such as making a custody decision without best-interest findings.

When the Court of Appeals denies a motion for peremptory reversal (or when the attorney does not file such a motion), and the case languishes on the Court of Appeals's regular custody docket for eight to twelve months or longer, there is a risk that the established custodial environment could shift from the parent appealing the trial judge's decision to the parent erroneously granted custody. How long this shift takes depends on the facts in each case. There is not a bright-line rule under the Child Custody Act. Courts have held that periods of eleven months or even two years may not be enough time to change the established custodial environment, but four years is an appreciable amount of time.

INTERSTATE AND INTERNATIONAL CUSTODY ISSUES HEIGHTEN CASES' COMPLEXITY AND PARENTS' EMOTIONS

Interstate and international custody cases have so many facets; only a brief mention can be made here. There are multiple state and federal statutes governing these types of cases. The laws of other states and foreign nations also play a role. Problems often arise in deciding which state or which country will make the custody decision. Michigan's Uniform Child-Custody Jurisdiction and Enforcement Act (UCCJEA) says a child's home state has the jurisdiction to make an initial custody decision or decide a custody dispute. Similarly, under the Hague Abduction Convention, a child's "habitual residence" should be the nation to decide custody issues. Interstate and international custody cases are very time intensive for attorneys who take them on, particularly when a child has been kidnapped by the other parent, and the aggrieved parent must turn to the courts to seek the child's return.

In *Moreno v Zank*, the child was born in 2006 in Michigan. The parties' divorce decree called for joint custody, but the mother was prohibited from taking the child to Ecuador without notice to the father. In December 2009, the mother did just that. The father filled out a Hague Convention petition but never completed the process. In 2010, the mother allowed the father and his parents to visit the child in Ecuador. In the same year she obtained an ex parte order prohibiting the child from leaving the country, but the parties ultimately agreed to allow the child to visit Michigan for summer break. At the end of the summer, the father did not send the child back to Ecuador. Instead, he filed a petition for permanent custody, which was granted. Ten months later, the mother filed a Hague Convention petition. The district court held that the mother's initial abduction meant that Ecuador could not be the child's habitual residence. On appeal, the

Sixth Circuit reversed, holding the proper remedy for the mother's initial kidnapping was a Hague Convention case (and not the father's rekidnapping). The Sixth Circuit remanded the case to address the father's defenses to the child's habitual residence being Ecuador. "A district court may refuse to return a child otherwise required to be returned if the child objects to being returned and has attained an age and degree of maturity at which it is appropriate to take account of its views." Because these defenses are very fact intensive, the Sixth Circuit remanded for "specific and detailed fact-finding by the district court."

International cases can take years to finally determine which nation or state decides custody. In Friedrich v Friedrich, the child was five years old when he was sent back to Germany. Imagine how strange that would have been for that child! In Monasky v Taglieri, the little girl was sent back to Italy two years into the five-year case. That must be very traumatic for a child. In fact, the United States Supreme Court in Abbott v Abbott held that child abduction is child abuse.

—**JEANNE HANNAH,** attorney, Traverse City, MI

UNRESOLVED ISSUES IN CHILD CUSTODY DECISIONS

TRIAL JUDGES FAILING TO FULLY EXAMINE BEST INTERESTS OF THE CHILD AFTER FULL CUSTODY TRIAL

In initial custody cases, such as divorce cases, judges typically enter a temporary or interim order that will govern the family's life while the divorce litigation ensues. As discussed earlier, the trial judge should not enter such an interim or temporary order without hearing evidence and making findings under the Child Custody Act. In *Lech v Lech*, the trial judge did the temporary order exactly right by hearing evidence and making findings on the best interests before issuing the temporary order. Even though the father's parenting time with the parties' six-year-old daughter was limited, the referee and trial judge acknowledged that the parties would work toward having equal parenting time once the father attended therapy for depression. The problem in the custody case did not arise until the end of the divorce trial, after the father demonstrated that he had benefitted from therapy. Rather than examining all the evidence and evaluating the best interests, the trial judge required the father to demonstrate the *Vodvarka* threshold of proper cause or change of circumstances to modify the temporary order. This threshold burden should not have been placed on the father, as the custody order was temporary and based on an abbreviated presentation of evidence early in the case. Instead, the trial judge found that the father had not met the threshold and so did not consider the child's best interests at all. The Court of Appeals affirmed the trial judge, distinguishing the cases that state that the parent is not required to prove the threshold when custody is decided in an original custody order following a temporary order. The court reasoned that those published decisions did not involve the trial judge hearing evidence to make that initial temporary ruling.

CONCLUSORY FINDINGS ON THE ESTABLISHED CUSTODIAL ENVIRONMENT

Many trial judges make findings on the established custodial environment by simply declaring that the mother or the father has the established custodial environment or that both parents have an established custodial environment. But that statement alone is not actually a factual finding; it's a conclusion. Trial judges should make more detailed findings about the facts to support their decisions on the established custodial environment. The trial judge should talk about the facts from the evidentiary record that support each element: guidance, discipline, necessities of life, and parental comfort.

For example, evidence that the child always turns to one parent when they are not feeling well, are upset about something, or want advice would relate to the "guidance" aspect of the established custodial environment. That one parent is a disciplinarian while the other has no rules in their house would support the "discipline" element.

When trial judges base their decisions on a conclusion about the established custodial environment without doing a deep dive into the facts that came out during trial, there is no way to know whether that decision was right or wrong. Leaving this important question unanswered impacts the judge's entire analysis of the case going forward, affecting the burden of proof as discussed above.

MORE PROBLEMS RELATED TO THE ESTABLISHED CUSTODIAL ENVIRONMENT

There are many appellate cases that discuss the "established custodial environment" and whether there has been an appreciable time that a child has looked to one parent or another for guidance, discipline, necessities of life, and comfort. However, judges don't often reach the next part of the Child Custody Act's standard: "The age of the child, the physical environment, and the inclination of the custodian and the child as to permanency of the relationship shall also be considered."

Most cases simply cite the standard without engaging in an in-depth analysis of the facts to support it. However, one case provides an example of facts that impact the inclination of the parent and child as to the permanency of the relationship. In *Aguilar v Aguilar*, the trial judge relied on the following facts to find that there was permanency in the relationship between the mother and the children: "[The mother] was the primary caretaker of the children before the divorce was filed. She took maternity leave when they were born, she provided for their daily care, and she took them to doctor appointments. In contrast, [the father] only became more active in their lives after [the mother] filed for divorce." Based on these facts, the trial judge concluded that the children were still young and would be looking for a parent to provide care on a regular basis. The Court of Appeals agreed with the trial judge's decision that the parent would be the mother.

DEFERENCE TO TRIAL COURT DECISIONS BASED ON TRANSCRIPTS OF REFEREE HEARINGS

There is a grave concern that arises when a trial judge limits their de novo review of an FOC referee recommendation to the transcripts of the referee hearing rather than taking live testimony. Although this practice is permitted by the court rules, it allows the trial judge to make credibility findings without observing the witnesses, based solely on a cold record—the transcripts from the referee hearing and the documents presented to the referee. By reading the transcript, the trial judge loses the normal cues available in an evidentiary hearing, such as witness behavior on the stand, cadence of speech, tone of voice, nervousness, and other signals that the witness is lying. This is no different than the Court of Appeals reviewing the record from the trial court proceeding, and yet the Court of Appeals must give deference to the trial judge's fact findings and credibility determinations. This issue should be raised on appeal whenever the trial judge does not hear live testimony but relies only on the referee transcripts and documentary evidence.

THE CHILD INTERVIEW

Although there are many published decisions that discuss child interviews, there are still contradictory decisions from the Court of Appeals on whether or when a child interview is necessary. According to the Child Custody Act, the trial judge must consider the reasonable preference of the child if the child is old enough to express a preference. There are many cases that say a six-year-old is old enough. A particularly mature child could express a preference at an even younger age. But certainly, by the time a child is six years old, the trial judge should at least hold a private interview (known as an in-camera or in-chambers interview) with the child to first make the determination of whether the child is old enough to express a preference and then find out what that child's reasonable preference is.

Sometimes, trial judges misuse child interviews to resolve factual disputes. For instance, in *Foskett v Foskett*, the trial judge interviewed the parties' three children (ages thirteen, eleven, and eight). Before the interview, the trial judge invited the parties to "present questions that it would ask the children" and informed them that "it would also ask the children about plaintiff's drinking habits, alleged verbal abuse, the frequency of the presence of the police at the home, as well as the source of clothing for the children." The Court of Appeals, searching for an explanation for the trial judge's decision to change custody, observed that "after the trial court spoke with the children in camera, the trial court suddenly concluded that the mother was 'cursed with a very volatile temper,' was 'verbally abusive,' and had 'a mental problem,' and that it "appears domestic violence plagues the mother's home environment." None of this information could be gleaned from the custody trial record. Accordingly, the Court of Appeals stated the "only conceivable explanation to account for the stark difference between the evidence presented on the record ...

is the intervening in-camera interview with the children that was not, in any way, made part of the reviewable record." The Court of Appeals held that in order to "provide for meaningful appellate review" of the trial judge's decision, "there must be a modicum of extraneous testimony on the record that would, at the very least, support a reasonable inference attesting to the trustworthiness and, indeed, the veracity of the information obtained through the in-camera interview with the children." The Court of Appeals reversed the trial judge's change of custody, noting the impact of such an unsupported decision on the children:

> [D]ecisions that will profoundly affect the lives and well-being
> of children cannot be left to little more than pure chance. These
> critical decisions must be subject to meaningful appellate review.

—HON. KIRSTEN FRANK KELLY, *Foskett v Foskett*

REASONABLENESS OF CHILD'S PREFERENCE

Should a judge be able to decide that a child's preference is not reasonable without ever speaking with the child? The Court of Appeals said that was OK in *Maier v Maier*, but I question the practice. According to the Child Custody Act, the only time a child should not be allowed to share a preference is when the child is not old enough to state a reasonable preference. In *Maier*, the trial judge concluded, and the Court of Appeals agreed, that the child's preference was not reasonable because the trial judge found that the child was emotionally distressed and potentially had been coached by his mother. Yet without giving a child the opportunity to speak directly with the judge, how could he or she state a preference? Giving the child a personal meeting with the trial judge also allows the child to express his or her preference orally and not in writing, thus allowing clear communication unimpeded by the child's written communication skills.

CONSIDERING EACH INDIVIDUAL CHILD'S BEST INTERESTS.

Sometimes trial judges conduct best-interest analyses but do not consider each child individually, instead lumping all the children together. There is not clear authority requiring trial judges to consider each child individually, but based on the language of the Child Custody Act, it only seems fair. If there are two high schoolers in the family and two elementary school children, it might be appropriate to consider the children's best interests based on classification by how old they are, but in other cases, it may be necessary to consider each child's relationships with their parents separately. The established custodial environment could even be different for each child based on whom that individual child looks to for guidance, discipline, necessities of life, and parental comfort.

There is not clear authority requiring trial judges to consider each child individually, but based on the language of the Child Custody Act, it only seems fair.

Two published cases touch on the interplay of keeping siblings together while also considering the children's best interests individually. In *Wiechmann v Wiechmann*, the parties had four children—two older children and two younger twins. The trial judge granted custody of the older children to the father and custody of the younger twins to the mother. The mother appealed, and the Court of Appeals affirmed because the trial judge had considered the best interests of each child individually. However, the Court of Appeals also observed:

"This Court appreciates the importance of attempting to keep siblings together. The sibling bond and the potentially detrimental effects of physically severing that bond should be seriously considered in custody cases where the children likely have already experienced serious disruption in their lives as well as a sense of deep personal loss. Ultimately, however, it is the best interests of each individual child that will control the custody decision."

In addition, the Court of Appeals in *Foskett v Foskett* reversed the trial judge's decision to change custody of three children (ages thirteen, eleven, and eight) because the evidence only supported that it was in the oldest child's best interests for the father to have custody. Together, these cases suggest an individualized analysis is necessary for the children's best interests.

ARE STAY-AT-HOME PARENTS FAVORED BY JUDGES?

There is also a question as to how a trial judge should consider a child's established custodial environment with a parent who works outside of the home. In *Bofysil v Bofysil*, two women married and had a child together. Upon their divorce, the trial judge found that the young child had a better "established custodial environment" with the parent who acted as the "stay-at-home mother" based on the amount of time they were able to spend together, while the other mother was the "working parent." The Court of Appeals noted the courts cannot automatically discount the child's established custodial environment with a working parent simply because that parent leaves for work while the other parent stays home. Although one parent worked outside the home, "she arranged her schedule to maximize her time home during [the child's] waking hours." Although the two parents took care of the child in different ways and in respect to different aspects of the child's life, she had a custodial relationship with both of her mothers. It was wrong for the trial judge to fault the working parent for being employed full time.

KEY TAKEAWAYS

- The purpose of the Child Custody Act is to avoid disruptions of the child's <u>established custodial environment</u> *unless* there is a very compelling reason.

- Before making a best-interest finding, the trial court *must determine* which parent has the established custodial environment—this finding determines the burden of proof the judge must apply to the custody decision.

- A trial court should make <u>detailed findings</u> as to the established custodial environment—not simply declare that it exists with one parent.

- When a case is remanded to a trial court, the judge must consider <u>up-to-date evidence.</u>

- When trial courts make legal errors in custody cases, the Court of Appeals should <u>peremptorily reverse</u> these decisions so that the case is correctly decided in a timely manner.

RESOURCES FOR CHAPTER TWO

ESTABLISHED CUSTODIAL ENVIRONMENT

Aguilar v Aguilar, unpublished per curiam opinion, issued Dec 19, 2019 (Docket No. 347338).

Baker v Baker, 411 Mich 567; 309 NW2d 532 (1980).

Bofysil v Bofysil, 322 Mich App 232; 956 NW2d 544 (2020).

Bowers v Bowers, 198 Mich App 320; 497 NW2d 602 (1993).

Dixon v Dixon, unpublished per curiam opinion of Court of Appeals, issued June 14, 2016 (Docket No. 329914).

Foskett v Foskett, 247 Mich App 1; 634 NW2d 363 (2001).

Gagne v Ordway, unpublished per curiam opinion of Court of Appeals, issued August 16, 2002 (Docket No. 235425).

Kessler v Kessler, 295 Mich App 54; 811 NW2d 39 (2011).

Landon v Shelton, unpublished per curiam opinion of Court of Appeals, issued December 21, 2010 (Docket No. 297064).

Lenz v Neal, unpublished per curiam opinion of Court of Appeals, issued September 3, 1999 (Docket No. 217165).

Mills v Mills, unpublished per curiam opinion of Court of Appeals, issued March 17, 1998 (Docket No. 195531).

Zori v Zori, unpublished per curiam opinion of Court of Appeals, issued December 22, 2011 (Docket No. 304153).

MCL 722.27(1)(c).

CUSTODY THRESHOLD

Kessler v Kessler, 295 Mich App 54; 811 NW2d 39 (2011).

Lech v Lech, unpublished per curiam opinion of Court of Appeals, issued June 10, 2021 (Docket No. 355632).

Thompson v Thompson, 261 Mich App 353; 683 NW2d 250 (2004).

Vodvarka v Grasmeyer, 259 Mich App 499; 675 NW2d 847 (2003).

LEGAL PROCEDURE

Fletcher v Fletcher, 447 Mich 871; 526 NW2d 889 (1994).

Grooms v Huntzinger, 504 Mich 966; 933 NW2d 41 (2019).

Homes v Holmes, unpublished order of the Court of Appeals, issued April 2, 2019 (Docket No. 347410).

Marik v Marik, 325 Mich App 353; 925 NW2d 885 (2018).

Peck v Peck, unpublished per curiam opinion of Court of Appeals, issued September 8, 2012 (Docket No. 306329).

Pierron v Pierron, 282 Mich App 222; 765 NW2d 345 (2009).

MCR 3.215(F).

BEST INTEREST FACTORS

Freeman v Freeman, 163 Mich App 493; 414 NW2d 914 (1987).

Holmes v Holmes, unpublished per curiam opinion of Court of Appeals, issued September 1, 2018 (Docket No. 341025).

Riemer v Johnson, 311 Mich App 632; 876 NW2d 279 (2015).

Wiechmann v Wiechmann, 212 Mich App 436; 538 NW2d 57 (1995).

MCL 722.23.

CHILD INTERVIEW

Kubicki v Sharp, 306 Mich App 525; 858 NW2d 57 (2014).

Maier v Maier, 311 Mich App 218; 874 NW2d 725 (2015).

HAGUE CONVENTION CASES

Abbott v Abbott, 560 US 1; 130 S Ct 1983; 176 L Ed 2d 789 (2010).

Friedrich v Friedrich, 983 F2d 1396 (CA 6, 1993).

Monasky v Taglieri, 589 US ___; 140 S Ct 719; 206 L Ed 2d 9 (2020).

Moreno v Zank, 895 F3d 917 (CA 6, 2018).

CHAPTER THREE

CHILD CUSTODY MODIFICATION

Postjudgment Litigation Is Rife with Errors

•   •   •

THE PURPOSE OF CHILD CUSTODY MODIFICATIONS

Postjudgment custody modification is based on the same premise as initial custody decisions: the best interests of the child. Trial judges should avoid unnecessary disruptions to a child's life. The Supreme Court has said the Child Custody Act was designed to "erect a barrier against removal of a child from an established custodial environment and to minimize unwarranted and disruptive changes of custody orders."

QUICK LEGAL SUMMARY OF CHILD CUSTODY MODIFICATIONS

A parent who wants to modify an existing custody order must file a motion alleging facts that amount to **proper cause** or a **change of circumstances**. Depending on the extent of the modification (that is, how the proposed change alters the number of days the child spends with each parent), different threshold standards apply.

The threshold to modify custody comes from *Vodvarka v Grasmeyer*. The *Vodvarka* threshold requires the basis for the requested modification to significantly impact the child's life under at least one of the best-interest factors in the Child Custody Act. According to *Vodvarka*, "since the entry of the last custody order, the conditions surrounding custody of the child, which have or could have a *significant* effect on the child's well-being, [must] have materially changed." Normal life changes (such as the child getting older, the parent remarrying, the parent changing jobs) are not sufficient. The courts use less stringent threshold standards for parenting-time modifications, called the *Shade* standard after *Shade v Wright*, as discussed in chapter 6.

After deciding whether the allegations in the motion surpass the *Vodvarka* threshold, judges can then consider the evidence regarding the established custodial environment and the best interests of the child, just as they do in initial custody decisions, as discussed in chapter 2. Deciding whether the allegations satisfy the *Vodvarka* threshold for custody or the lesser standards for parenting time will influence the ultimate outcome of the case in at least two significant ways. First, knowing which threshold applies could affect whether the trial judge must find **clear and convincing evidence** in favor of modification or if the lesser **burden of proof, preponderance of the evidence,** is appropriate. Second, custody orders are appealable by right while parenting-time orders are only appealable by application for leave. The difference between the two types of appeals is discussed in chapter 1.

PROBLEM AREAS IN CHILD CUSTODY MODIFICATION DECISIONS

EXPANDING THE DE NOVO HEARING BEYOND THE OBJECTION TO THE REFEREE RECOMMENDATION

Once the referee issues its recommendation for custody and parenting time, either party can file an objection within twenty-one days. According to court rule, the objection must provide a "clear and concise statement" that specifically identifies each fact and application of the law contested by the parent. The idea is that the de novo hearing before the trial judge will focus on those facts and issues that were contained in the objection. However, many times one party will make a generalized objection that does not inform the other parent what will be covered at the de novo hearing. That occurred in *Mansfield v Mansfield*. The referee made a recommendation on parenting time and custody, and the father objected by merely stating that he did not object to any of the referee's factual findings but instead complained that the referee did not find that a change of custody to him would be in the child's best interests. The mother filed a motion to strike the objection for lack of specificity, but the trial judge denied her motion and allowed the father to proceed with the de novo hearing to challenge the referee's custody recommendation. The Court of Appeals affirmed that procedural maneuver, stating: "[The mother] was aware of the nature of [the father]'s objection before the hearing" and so was not prejudiced. This ruling seems to remove the notion of fair play when the nonobjecting party does not know how to prepare for the de novo hearing.

Even worse, the Court of Appeals has endorsed this practice in *Kostreva v Kostreva*, a case where the father objected to a referee recommendation solely on attorney fees, and the mother did not file her own objection as to the parenting-time/passport ruling. But after the close of proofs at the de novo hearing on the father's objection, the trial judge sua sponte decided to address the referee's passport recommendation and subsequently ruled against the father on that point. Once again, the Court of Appeals affirmed that procedural maneuver, stating that MCR 3.215 only governed a party's objections, but the trial judge is authorized at the de novo hearing to hear "any matter that has been the subject of the referee hearing."

APPLYING THE WRONG THRESHOLD STANDARD

There have been numerous cases where trial judges apply the wrong threshold standard. When trial judges claim they are simply modifying parenting time, but the results change the child's established custodial environment, trial judges inevitably apply the wrong threshold standard.

In *Lieberman v Orr*, the children lived with their mother in Clinton County and exercised parenting time with their father in Midland County. Based on the existing parenting-time order, the children were with their mother 225 overnights per year and with their father 140 overnights. The father filed a motion to modify parenting time and change schools from DeWitt to Midland. The mother asked the trial judge to dismiss the petition because the father had failed to meet the threshold for reopening the custody order. The trial judge focused on the school issue and concluded that, because there was an established custodial environment with both parents, the preponderance of the evidence standard applied. The trial judge acknowledged the father's motion raised normal life changes, which the judge said only required the court to apply the *Shade* threshold. The trial judge granted the father's motion to modify parenting time, based on a preponderance of the evidence in favor of Midland schools. She reasoned that she was simply "flipping" the parenting-time schedules so that father would now have 225 overnights and mother would have 140 overnights.

The Court of Appeals vacated the trial judge's decision in *Lieberman* because she should have applied the *Vodvarka* standard, and not the lesser *Shade* standard, to determine whether the father had alleged proper cause or change in circumstances to justify a modification of parenting time. The opinion called the father's motion an attempt to change primary physical custody under the guise of a change in parenting time. The Court further held that the change in overnights meant that the mother was losing her ability to remain involved in day-to-day activities during the school year. The drastic change in overnights defied the idea that the mother was the "primary" physical custodian of the children. Thus, the Court of Appeals held that the trial judge should have required the father to present clear and convincing evidence that the modification was in the children's best interests.

> **PRACTICE TIP:** *Trial attorneys can encourage trial judges to follow the proper steps in modifying a custody order by following the same structure in their briefs and closing arguments. Clearly state your position on the established custodial environment and the appropriate burden of proof before advocating in your client's favor on the best-interest factors.*

NIK'S STORY:
Kidnapper Mom Awarded Custody When Court Used the Wrong Standard

Nik lived in North Dakota, but the Clinton County judge awarded him sole legal and physical custody of his daughter after the mother kidnapped her. Nik, his daughter, Nik's wife, and a younger child lived in North Dakota for five years. Nik's daughter came to Michigan for summers and other holidays. During one summer visit, the mom asked to change custody. Because she had moved to Detroit, a different judge heard the motion. The judge changed custody using the wrong standard, and the Court of Appeals reversed.

The judge's ruling came at the end of summer. Due to the distance, Nik only saw his daughter one time during that summer and following school year. She also had a tough time adjusting to her new school. The judge's decision had hurt her emotionally and academically.

The case was also very hard on Nik's whole family, who missed her terribly. But it was most difficult for Nik's younger daughter, who lost her big sister.

USING THE WRONG BURDEN OF PROOF TO MODIFY CUSTODY

Some trial judges identify the correct threshold but then apply the wrong burden of proof to the custody modification decision. Changing a child's environment from one parent to the other will have a significant impact on a child's day-to-day living. Still, many trial judges have applied a preponderance standard to custody changes when they should have applied a clear and convincing standard because the modification would change who the child looked to for parental comfort, guidance, discipline, and the necessities of life. When a trial judge uses the wrong burden of proof, it uproots the child's life without sufficient evidence to prove doing so is in the child's best interests.

> *Changing a child's environment from one parent to the other will have a significant impact on a child's day-to-day living.*

The father in *Palmer* (see "Nik's Story") had primary physical custody of the child for many years in North Dakota. The trial judge changed custody to the mother in Michigan after finding that the parties shared a joint established custodial environment and applying the lower preponderance of the evidence standard to its best-interest analysis. The father filed an appeal by right, along with a motion for **peremptory reversal**. The Court of Appeals denied that motion even though the trial judge had plainly made a legal error by applying the lower burden of proof. Once the appeal was fully briefed and argued, a different panel of the Court of Appeals reversed the trial judge's decision and remanded the case so the trial judge could redo her best-interest analysis using the clear and convincing evidence standard.

JUDGES ENTERING TEMPORARY ORDER WITHOUT EVIDENCE OR FACT-FINDINGS

In *Jacob* (discussed in chapter 1), the trial judge suspended the father's parenting time based on allegations after an incident at the airport. The father decided to take the children on a last-minute vacation, and his daughter reacted badly. She called the **Lawyer Guardian Ad Litem (L-GAL)**, who instructed the daughter to leave her family and go to the bathroom so that the L-GAL could speak to her privately. In the meantime, the father did not know where his daughter was. The L-GAL filed an emergency motion to suspend the father's parenting time, and the trial judge relied on the L-GAL's statements to grant the motion without an evidentiary hearing or fact findings to support the decision. During the litigation, the trial judge entered five more orders without an evidentiary hearing or fact findings. The Court of Appeals vacated all six orders because they were based on "legal defects" and "unfounded" allegations. The failure to conduct an evidentiary hearing deprived the father of due process of law.

> *[I]t is important that lower courts follow the correct procedure when modifying a child's established custodial environment. As the statutory scheme reflects, doing so is serious business.*

—HON. JUSTICE ELIZABETH CLEMENT,
concurring opinion in *O'Brien v D'Annunzio*

WHEN THE PARENTS ARE PRACTICALLY EQUAL ON ALL BEST-INTEREST FACTORS

What happens when everyone agrees a change must be made, but the parents are equal on the best-interest factors? What is a judge to do when a change must be made, but neither party can prove their situation is better by clear and convincing evidence? In *Griffin v Griffin*, the parents lived in different states—the father lived in Holt, Michigan, and the mother lived in Illinois. Despite the distance, the parents had equal parenting time with their young child. However, as kindergarten approached, both parents filed motions to modify custody. The trial judge found that the child had an established custodial environment with both parents but then granted the change of custody in favor of the mother, using the preponderance standard when the clear and convincing standard should have applied. In reversing the trial judge, the Court of Appeals expressed sympathy to the judge's position, saying the judge was:

> [F]aced with a somewhat unique problem: Everyone agreed that maintaining the current custodial arrangement was not in the child's best interests…. [Yet] it is arguable that when compared to each other, neither [the father]'s proposed change nor [the mother]'s proposed change was, by clear and convincing evidence, superior to the other's proposal.

The Court of Appeals concluded that the Child Custody Act "does not require that one parent's proposed change must be better than the other parent's proposal by a clear and convincing evidence standard," only that the change is in the child's best interests "when compared to the status quo." Thus, when compared to the status quo of equally shared time, the "key is that the court must first find by clear and convincing evidence that the new custodial arrangement is in the child's best interests."

Judge Christopher Murray dissented from the *Griffin* decision. He observed that the trial judge "recognized that a change had to be made" because the child was starting kindergarten and could no longer live with both parents on alternative weeks. Judge Murray commented, "The child's best interests could only be served by altering the existing custody arrangement—sending him to a school where he would miss two weeks of classes for every two weeks attended would be nonsensical and would not be in his best interests as a matter of law." Judge Murray stated that the trial judge only had two options in this situation:

(1) enter an order that did not change the established custodial environment and find by a preponderance of the evidence that the child's best interests demanded that he live with one of the parties during the school year; or (2) enter an order changing the established custodial environment and find by clear and convincing evidence that the child's best interests could only be served by awarding either plaintiff or defendant custody of the child during the school year.

Unfortunately, both the majority and dissenting opinions leave something to be desired. Requiring the trial judge to compare the parent's proposed modification to the status quo seems confusing. However, the alternative is that parents who are otherwise equal on all factors could have the balance tip one way or the other based on the slightest difference between their homes or parenting styles.

CUSTODY FINDINGS AGAINST THE GREAT WEIGHT OF THE EVIDENCE

The Court of Appeals must defer to the trial judge's fact findings and credibility determinations. The trial judge's opinion of the witnesses' testimony typically carries through the appellate decision. Though it is rare, the Court of Appeals occasionally does reverse the trial judge's factual findings. In *Lasley v Miller*, the mother had a short-term relationship with a man who disappeared once she became pregnant. Eventually, the cost of raising a child as a single parent pushed her to file a paternity action for child support. Then when her daughter was four, the father married and finally decided he wanted to have parenting time with his daughter. Not surprisingly, the parents did not get along very well, and the father continuously complained about every decision the mother made. The father filed a custody motion based on allegations that the mother denied parenting time on a few occasions, contentious parenting time exchanges, and the mother's decision to homeschool the child for the year before kindergarten. The trial judge completely inverted custody, taking sole legal and physical custody from the mother and giving it to the father, limiting the mother to parenting time on alternating weekends and a midweek visit.

The Court of Appeals reversed the trial judge's custody decision, holding that the judge's fact findings were against the great weight of the evidence. The trial judge's fact findings penalized the mother, who had sole legal custody, for changing the child's preschool without the father's consent. As sole legal custodian, she had every right to do so. The Court of Appeals disagreed with the trial judge's fact findings on several other grounds as well. For instance, the trial judge found that best-interest factor (j)—the willingness of the parent to facilitate a parent-child relationship with the other parent—favored the father because the trial judge was convinced the mother had coached the child before a court-ordered psychologist's meeting. The Court of Appeals disagreed because even the psychologist noted that she did not believe coaching had occurred. The Court of Appeals further observed that the father "continually baited [the mother] and created unnecessary problems." From the evidence at trial, it seemed that the father was never satisfied with the parenting time he was awarded and "continually harassed [the mother] with motions to change custody" and expand his parenting time, filing them as quickly as three weeks after his previous motion was denied.

The Court of Appeals also disagreed with the trial judge that factor (l)—any other factor—favored the father for similar reasons. The trial judge found that the mother had alienated the child from her father and had coached the child before she met with the psychologist. The Court of Appeals found no evidence to support parental alienation. Once again, the Court of Appeals observed that the father's extreme litigiousness (six motions within eighteen months) demonstrated that he was obsessed with winning. Based on these and other erroneous factual findings, the Court of Appeals reversed the trial judge's custody decision and remanded the case for the judge to redetermine custody.

DELAY BETWEEN EX PARTE CUSTODY MODIFICATION AND FINAL ORDER

As discussed in chapter 1, postjudgment modification cases experience substantial delays from the motion's filing to the final decision. This is particularly problematic when the trial judge enters an interim, ex parte, or temporary modification order that becomes the status quo for the child while the modification request is pending. For example, in *O'Brien v D'Annunzio*, fifteen months went by between the time the trial judge entered the ex parte order, granting the father's request for full physical custody and suspending the mother's parenting time, and the final custody decision after an evidentiary hearing. Sadly, this is a very common scenario in family courts around the state. The parent who is on the bad end of the temporary custody order will have a very difficult time reinstating the prior order at the end of the case, even though the trial judge's initial ex parte decision was erroneous and colored the trial judge's view of the parties as the case slowly progressed through the court proceedings. The situation is sad for the child and parent when a so-called temporary custody order changes the child's **established custodial environment.**

ALLEGATIONS THAT A PARENT HAS MENTAL HEALTH ISSUES REQUIRE CUSTODY CHANGES

There are many cases where a trial judge changes custody from one parent—usually the mother—to another—most often the father—based on allegations that the custodial parent's mental illness impacts their ability to parent their child. Although there is a published decision that says it is inappropriate to rely on unsupported allegations of mental illness to change custody, the problem is still occurring in family law courts throughout the state.

In *Pennington v Pennington*, the trial judge changed custody from the mother to the father after the mother raised concerns that the father sexually abused their young daughter. In response, the father claimed that the mother was mentally ill and excluding him from his daughter's life. However, the father presented no evidence of mental illness other than his personal opinion and a CPS investigator's testimony. The investigator believed the mother was seeking "too much" medical care for the child because physicians examining her had not found any evidence of abuse. The Court of Appeals issued a published opinion holding there had not been enough evidence admitted proving the mother's mental health. The Court stated, "Defendant, however, offered no evidence that plaintiff was mentally ill; the only evidence offered purportedly demonstrating plaintiff's 'mental illness,' apart from defendant's opinion, was the testimony of the CPS investigator.... The CPS investigator, however, is not a doctor and did not testify that she had any medical expertise. Defendant, in fact, offered no medical evidence to support his theory that plaintiff was medically ill ..."

In *O'Brien*, the trial judge decided the mother's mental health based on the father's allegations, even though the professional witnesses who examined the mother testified that she did not have a mental illness.

As Judge Gleicher noted in her dissent, the trial judge "made up her mind at the outset of the proceedings and simply disregarded the bulk of the evidence—particularly that provided by professionals..." Instead the trial judge found that the mother was emotionally unstable, and due to her instability, was "physically and emotionally abusive" to her children such that "parenting time with their mother would endanger the children's physical, mental, or emotional health."

Trial judges continue to change custody based on a supposed mental illness without medical proof, yet the Court of Appeals has repeatedly disregarded *Pennington*'s dictates. In each of its post-*Pennington* decisions, the Court of Appeals has found some way to distinguish *Pennington* and allow unsubstantiated evidence of mental illness to form the primary grounds for a change of custody.

Trial judges and the Court of Appeals not following binding decisions is certainly frustrating for attorneys and parties alike. Modifying custody without proof of a substantiated mental illness and without considering whether reasonable accommodations could be made for the parent's mental health condition is also bad for the children unceremoniously removed from their established custodial environments without proper evidence to support that change.

> **PRACTICE TIP:** *When the other party raises mental health concerns, you may need to request psychological evaluations, submit medical records, or present a treating therapist as an expert witness to show that your client's mental health condition is well controlled and does not negatively impact their ability to parent the child. Alternatively, you may also object to a lay witness's ability to testify to a medical condition or diagnosis. This will push trial judges toward requiring medical evidence to substantiate mental illness.*

PARENTAL ALIENATION AS REASON
TO CHANGE CUSTODY

Allegations of "parental alienation" frequently arise in high-conflict custody cases. There has been a dispute among experts about whether "parental alienation syndrome" exists as a clinical diagnosis. However, in the legal context, parental alienation occurs when "a child will not acknowledge a single positive thing about the other parent" and "acts by a parent that were intended to distance the child emotionally from the other parent." Whether a parent is alienating a child from their other parent is relevant to at least one of the best interest factors: factor (j), the "willingness and ability of each of the parties to facilitate and encourage a close and continuing parent-child relationship between the child and the other parent or the child and the parents."

In *Martin v Martin*, the Court of Appeals published a custody decision involving parental alienation where the mother failed to comply with the parenting-time schedule and taught the children false information about their father. The trial judge changed custody from the mother to the father and ordered that the mother could only have supervised parenting time with the parties' remaining minor child. The Court of Appeals affirmed the trial judge's decision to consider the alienation under the Child Custody Act's best-interest factors. The Court of Appeals also rejected the mother's argument that parental alienation is "junk science." The Court of Appeals acknowledged in a footnote: "While there may be a dispute in the scientific community about whether there is a diagnosable, pathological condition called parental alienation syndrome ... there is no reasonable dispute that high-conflict custody disputes frequently involve acts by one parent designed to obstruct or sabotage the opposing parent's relationship with the child."

Having been a family law attorney since 1967, the biggest shift I have seen is in how overnights are used to calculate child support. The changes in the Michigan Child Support Formula have resulted in a massive proliferation of custody and parenting-time disputes, as some parents try to increase their overnights to either increase what they receive in child support or reduce their child support obligation. It would be better for Michigan families and children to tie child support to one parent's need and the other parent's ability to pay rather than how many overnights the parent has with their children. If that sort of change were implemented, then not only would the judges' caseloads be reduced, but they could spend more time on what was best for the kids."

—**ROSS STANCATI**, attorney, Kalamazoo, MI

UNRESOLVED ISSUES IN CHILD CUSTODY MODIFICATION DECISIONS

DISPUTE ON THRESHOLD FACTS

Normally trial judges can decide whether a custody motion passes the threshold on the pleadings alone. However, when there is a factual dispute between the parents over whether enough has occurred to warrant revisiting custody, an evidentiary hearing is necessary to resolve that dispute before the trial judge can make a good faith ruling on the motion. If the trial judge fails to hold an evidentiary hearing on the threshold, the Court of Appeals may reverse the decision and remand the case for want of further factual findings.

This occurred in *D'Itri v Bollinger*. The mother filed a motion to modify custody based on a long list of changes that she alleged significantly impacted her daughter's mental health, stemming from the death of her daughter's stepmother and the father's inability to cope with that loss. The father responded that, although the death of the stepmother did have an impact on him and the child, he always cared for the child and addressed her needs by feeding her healthy meals and by keeping sanitary living conditions and a clean house. He further accused the mother of "attempting to manipulate" the child. The trial judge dismissed the motion to modify and simply held that the mother had not satisfied the *Vodvarka* threshold. The Court of Appeals disagreed and held that, because the parties had a factual dispute on the threshold allegations, the trial judge was obligated to hold an evidentiary hearing on the threshold issue before she could make her fact findings on the existence of proper cause or change in circumstances. Unfortunately, the *D'Itri* case was unpublished, so trial courts are not bound to follow its ruling. The Court of Appeals should publish an opinion that states the law as laid out in *D'Itri*.

Similarly, in *Giordana v Giordana*, another unpublished opinion, the mother filed a motion to change custody, alleging the father physically abused the children. The father denied the allegations and claimed the mother was coaching the children. The trial judge found that the mother's allegations did not surpass the *Vodvarka* threshold and denied her motion. The Court of Appeals vacated, holding that the trial judge should have held an evidentiary hearing because there were contested factual issues on whether the father was physically abusive and whether the mother was coaching the children to make false accusations against the father.

PRACTICE TIP: *When filing an answer where the threshold facts are disputed, explicitly request an evidentiary hearing on the issue of proper cause or change of circumstances in your requested relief. This will preserve the issue and make it easier to address on appeal.*

RELEVANCE OF EVIDENCE FROM BEFORE
THE LAST CUSTODY ORDER

As discussed above, in deciding whether there is a change of circumstances or proper cause for the *Vodvarka* threshold standard, the
trial judges will only look at facts that occurred *after* the last custody
order. But many trial judges around the state limit the best-interest
evidence to the same period. The question is this: Can the trial judge
consider evidence that predates the last custody order as part of its
best-interest analysis?

The Court of Appeals addressed this problem head-on in the
unpublished decision of *Baird v Richmond*. There, the trial judge
refused to allow the father to present evidence about physical violence
between the mother and her boyfriend and the mother's and maternal
grandfather's substance abuse in the child's home because the events
occurred before the last custody order. The Court of Appeals reversed
the trial judge's decision. In doing so, the Court of Appeals recognized
that while a "trial court generally has the authority to limit the presentation of the evidence," *Vodvarka* recognized that this "limitation was
applicable only to the question of whether a change in circumstances
or proper cause exists." The Court of Appeals continued, saying there
is no "blanket limitation" against using preexisting evidence as part
of the trial judge's best-interest analysis.

> Indeed, such a restriction would be contrary to the point of
> determining a child's best interests. At a minimum, evidence
> of prior behaviors is necessary to determine whether a party
> is continuing to make bad decisions or working to improve
> their life. Certainly, nothing prevents the trial court from
> weighing the evidence of recent behaviors more heavily.
> Indeed, it would seem quite reasonable to do so. The court

may not, however, draw an arbitrary temporal line and refuse to consider any behaviors that occurred before that time. Rather, the trial court must consider all evidence that might be relevant to the best-interests determination.

The Court held that the trial judge "erred when it refused to consider evidence of past conduct in assessing whether a change was in the child's best interests." The Court of Appeals reversed the trial judge's decision and remanded the case for a new evidentiary hearing, ruling that "because the findings were made on a truncated record, they are necessarily flawed."

The Court of Appeals correctly analyzed the law in *Baird v Richmond*. However, because trial judges around this state are still arbitrarily cutting off the parent's presentation of evidence, and because the appellate courts have been inconsistent about whether they will reverse the trial judge's decision, the Court of Appeals should include that legal analysis in a future published decision.

CHILDREN AND SOCIAL MEDIA

Another issue that comes up in postjudgment custody cases is the parents' ability to control their children's use of social media. There has not been a published custody opinion on this issue, but one unpublished custody case and a published delinquency case address the problem.

In *O'Brien* (discussed earlier), the mother repeatedly expressed concerns about her teenage daughter's use of Instagram and other social media applications. Both the father and the teen rebuffed her. Yet the mother was concerned because she had found inappropriate text messages on her daughter's cell phone: "How old r u"; "Your cute and I wanna seem them nudes mama"; "Dont tell me what to do bby girl." The trial judge criticized the mother for accessing her child's social media accounts. But Judge Gleicher, the dissenting judge, asserted that the mother was in the right to monitor her child's social media usage. She should be allowed to sign into their accounts and follow them to monitor for these kinds of messages.

In *In re JP*, a published juvenile delinquency case, the Court of Appeals addressed the "dangers of uncontrolled social media use by teenagers," particularly the Snapchat exchanges between several teenage girls about a male classmate. The Court noted that it is "reasonable for a school to condemn and punish misuse of social media and the potential for cyberbullying it represents. Children should be strongly encouraged to use digital media responsibly, to consider all the potential consequences of their words, and to refrain from any aggressive, inflammatory, or hurtful commentary."

The Court of Appeals should apply this logic to a published case involving parents monitoring their children's social media accounts. If children can be juvenile delinquents for what they do on social media, then most certainly parents should be able to monitor and control what their children are doing. Moreover, the parent's oversight is for the child's safety and protection, as the *O'Brien* facts suggest. A vigilant parent can prevent their child from becoming the victim of sex trafficking or misconduct. Using a parent's efforts to monitor a child's social media use to take away custody is not only offensive but dangerous.

> *Using a parent's efforts to monitor a child's social media use to take away custody is not only offensive but dangerous.*

HOLDING CUSTODY TRIAL BEFORE
MAKING A THRESHOLD FINDING

Trial judges often make the threshold fact findings on custody modification motions only after a full custody trial has occurred. This practice not only violates the Child Custody Act; it is also extremely harmful to families. The purpose of the Act is to avoid unnecessary disruptions to the custodial environment. Without an initial finding on proper cause or change of circumstances, the trial judge is exposing the family to disruption even in cases that do not meet the threshold, including the time, emotional impact, and expense of a custody trial, as well as any temporary or ex parte changes made while the case was pending (as discussed above). Under *Vodvarka*, the trial judge *must* make the threshold determination *before* it can even consider whether there is an established custodial environment or the best interests of the child. If the trial judge waits until after a custody hearing has already taken place to make the threshold determination, the trial judge may disrupt the child's established custodial environment where no such modification was necessary. By waiting until the end of a custody hearing, trial judges run the risk that what they learned will mold their views in reaching the threshold finding. Without making the crucial *Vodvarka* threshold findings early in the case, trial judges could cause serious damage and strain on a family—and, more importantly, on a minor child—that would have been completely unnecessary had the trial judge simply taken the time to make a threshold determination first.

Many times, the Court of Appeals gives trial judges a pass when they fail to make threshold findings at the proper time. The Court of Appeals might say that the trial judge's threshold finding was implicit or say the evidence offered at trial demonstrated a threshold-crossing event. In other cases, the trial judge does make a threshold finding but waits until after the custody trial is over to do so. In *Bauer v Waidelich*, the mother filed a motion to change legal custody (discussed in chapter 4) based on the parents' disagreements about their children's medical and educational needs. The trial judge did not make any findings on the threshold issue of proper cause or change in circumstances but instead launched into the custody trial. At the conclusion of that trial—which took nine days over many months—the trial judge briefly mentioned the threshold along with its analysis of the best-interest factors. Rather than making a threshold determination on the allegations included in the motion, the trial judge made his findings based on the evidence presented during nine days of trial. Although the Court of Appeals affirmed the trial judge's decision, this process should give great pause to parents and attorneys alike.

Should parents be put through the expense, time, and stress of a lengthy custody trial before the trial judge has even made a finding on the threshold of proper cause or change of circumstances? This procedure truly puts the cart before the horse. Indeed, if the trial judge wanted to hold a single evidentiary hearing on the disputed allegations for the threshold and the best-interest factors, the trial judge could take evidence on the threshold, pause the proceedings to make a finding as to whether the allegations passed the threshold for proper cause or change of circumstances, and then either end the hearing (no threshold) or continue the hearing (threshold passed) to take more evidence on the child's established custodial environment and best-interest factors.

Despite the published decisions requiring threshold decisions before revisiting custody, trial judges and the Court of Appeals have not consistently followed the law. In too many cases, trial judges are conducting entire custody trials before deciding the threshold question of whether there should be a custody trial at all. Because the Court of Appeals allows this to occur, the Supreme Court should weigh in on this issue, or the statute should be clarified.

RYAN'S STORY:

Mom's Move to Ohio Results in Custody Change

Ryan's daughter was connected to the local community—including both her extended family and sports teams. Her mom had commuted to Toledo for work for years. When the mom decided to marry, she sought to move to Ohio with the child. The judge granted the mom's request but also changed custody, even though such a motion had not been filed. The Court of Appeals sent the case back, warning the trial judge to follow the law for domicile and custody cases. Eventually, Ryan's daughter was allowed to move back to her father's home in Michigan, but it took a while. The judge did not accept that her order had been "vacated" on legal grounds.

Ryan was particularly frustrated by the judge holding court in chambers rather than on the record, which meant the parents only heard what happened after the fact. He felt the judge's decision had already been made, and they were just going through the motions.

The judge's decision also emboldened the mom to do "whatever she wanted," including keeping the child away from Ryan. The judge's decision hurt the child emotionally and academically; changing schools was a tough adjustment.

VACATING VERSUS REVERSING A
TRIAL JUDGE'S DECISION

When the Court of Appeals finds errors in a trial judge's decision-making, it will typically reverse or vacate the decision. The two terms have different meanings and should each have a different impact on how the trial judge handles the remand proceeding. But trial judges often read the terms interchangeably. Neither the Court of Appeals nor the Supreme Court has issued a binding explanation distinguishing the two terms. "Vacate" means "make void," while "reverse" means simply to "overturn." Therefore, the term "vacate" should be used when the trial judge's order is invalid for legal reasons—such as when the trial judge does not follow the law. Vacating a trial judge's order should reinstate the last valid custody order until the trial judge can complete the remand proceedings and correct their legal errors.

For example, in *Palmer v Anaya* (discussed above), the Court of Appeals vacated the trial judge's order for using the preponderance standard to change custody. Yet while the case was on remand, the daughter remained in Michigan with her mother—as directed by the erroneous custody order—rather than returning to her father's home in North Dakota. Unfortunately, many trial judges are reluctant to set the parties back to the last valid custody order even after their decisions have been vacated. This forces the families to live under a vacated custody order during the remand proceedings. (see "Ryan's Story"). Clarification from the appellate courts would help alleviate this situation by emphasizing that when an order is vacated, the family's life should be governed by the last valid order, not by the order that was vacated.

[The trial judge's] original error in entering the [interim custody order] without an evidentiary hearing ... justif[ies] vacating the [final custody] order and remanding the case. While vacating the order will undo the custody arrangement put in place by that order, the parties remain free to file new motions regarding custody.

—HON. JUSTICE ELIZABETH CLEMENT,
concurring opinion in *O'Brien v D'Annunzio*

In contrast, the term "reverse" applies when the findings are simply inadequate. Thus, when the appellate court reverses the trial judge's decision, the judge needs to review the facts and reach a new decision based on the appellate court's decision, but it need not void the custody order and start again. For example, in *Fletcher v Fletcher*, the Michigan Supreme Court reversed the trial judge's opinion, which placed too much emphasis on the issue of "fault" when weighing the best-interest factors. On remand, the appealed custody order should have remained in effect while the trial judge reexamined the evidence based on the appellate decision. When the appeals courts reverse on a specific factual finding, such as fault in *Fletcher*, the trial judge should follow the appellate court's instructions to properly analyze the facts and then decide whether their custody decision should remain or needs to change.

KEY TAKEAWAYS

- Like initial custody decisions, postjudgment custody modification is based on the best interests of the child.

- Before a trial court modifies custody, it must first determine whether the *Vodvarka* threshold is met, such that the basis for modification significantly impacts the child's life under at least one of the best-interest factors.

- For a parenting-time modification, a trial court should employ the less stringent *Shade* threshold.

- Which threshold standard applies impacts whether a trial court reviews the facts for clear and convincing evidence or a preponderance of the evidence.

- Custody orders are appealable by right, whereas parenting-time orders are only appealable by leave, so a trial court's mis-applying a threshold standard or burden of proof can severely uproot a child's life.

- If the judge fails to hold an evidentiary hearing to resolve a factual dispute on the threshold question, the Court of Appeals may remand for further factual findings.

RESOURCES FOR CHAPTER THREE

DOCKET DELAYS

Burmeister v Cole, unpublished per curiam opinion of Court of Appeals, issued September 27, 2016 (Docket No. 329899).

Landon v Shelton, unpublished per curiam opinion of Court of Appeals, issued December 21, 2010 (Docket No. 297064).

Lepage v Mertz, unpublished per curiam opinion of Court of Appeals, issued February 8, 2011 (Docket No. 299083).

Littman v Cohen, unpublished per curiam opinion of Court of Appeals, issued August 4, 2009 (Docket No. 288209).

O'Brien v D'Annunzio, unpublished per curiam opinion of Court of Appeals, issued February 27, 2020 (Docket No. 347830), rev'd by

__ Mich ___ (2021).

Pobanz v Pobanz, unpublished per curiam opinion of Court of Appeals, issued August 13, 2009 (Docket No. 291262).

Administrative Order No. 2013-12, Mich __ (2013).

MCR 3.210(C)(3).

FAILING TO FOLLOW THE LAW

Bowling v McCarrick, 318 Mich App 568; 899 NW2d 808 (2016).

Griffin v Griffin, 323 Mich App 110; 916 NW2d 292 (2018).

Lieberman v Orr, 319 Mich App 68; 900 NW2d 130 (2017).

Palmer v Anaya, unpublished per curiam opinion of Court of Appeals, March 26, 2019 (Docket No. 345368).

THRESHOLD ISSUES

Bauer v Waidelich, unpublished per curiam opinion of Court of Appeals, issued August 6, 2019 (Docket No. 345756).

Bonnell v Bonnell, unpublished per curiam opinion of Court of Appeals, issued May 13, 2014 (Docket No. 318445).

D'Itri v Bollinger, unpublished per curiam opinion of Court of Appeals, issued September 19, 2017 (Docket No. 337815).

Donald v Donald, unpublished per curiam opinion of Court of Appeals, issued November 6, 2003 (Docket No. 244782).

Giordana v Giordana, unpublished per curiam opinion of Court of Appeals, issued December 17, 2020 (Docket No. 354050).

Vodvarka v Grasmeyer, 259 Mich App 499, 675 NW2d 847 (2003).

MCR 3.210(C)(8).

DE NOVO HEARING

Kostreva v Kostreva, __ Mich App ___; ___ NW2d ___ (2021) (Docket Nos. 352029; 353316).

MCR 3.215(E)(4).

CUSTODY CONSIDERATIONS

Baker v Baker, 411 Mich 567; 309 NW2d 532 (1981).

Fletcher v Fletcher, 447 Mich 871; 526 NW2d 889 (1994).

Heid v Aaasulewski (After Remand), 209 Mich App 587; 532 NW2d 205 (1995).

In re JP, 330 Mich App 1; 944 NW2d 422 (2019).

Lasley v Miller, unpublished per curiam opinion of Court of Appeals, issued July 18, 2013 (Docket No. 313005).

Pennington v Pennington, 329 Mich App 562; 944 NW2d 131 (2019).

PARENTAL ALIENATION

In re Gorcyca, unpublished per curiam opinion of Court of Appeals, issued July 28, 2017 (Docket No. 152831).

Lopez-Negrete v Kariann, unpublished per curiam opinion of Court of Appeals, issued May 26, 2009 (Docket No. 286247).

Nichols, *Toward a Child-Centered Approach to Evaluating Claims of Alienation in High-Conflict Custody Disputes*, 112 Mich L Rev 663 (2014).

Nordhielm v Dapena-Baron, unpublished per curiam opinion of Court of Appeals, issued November 14, 2017 (Docket No. 335877).

ADDITIONAL RESOURCES

Speaker & Alberts, *What's the Difference Between "Reverse" and "Vacate"?* 47 Mich Fam L J, 3, 33 (Mar 2017).

Speaker Law Firm, *Top 11 Threshold Appeal Issues in Child Custody and Parenting Time Cases* < https://bit.ly/3pHEyBv> (accessed June 11, 2021).

CHAPTER FOUR

LEGAL CUSTODY

*Making Important Decisions That Affect
the Child's Health, Safety, and Welfare*

●　　　●　　　●

THE PURPOSE OF LEGAL CUSTODY

Each parent should be involved in the important decisions that affect
their child's life, including medical, educational, and religious issues.
Even when one parent has sole legal custody, the noncustodial parent is
still entitled to access to their children's medical and school information.

QUICK LEGAL SUMMARY OF LEGAL CUSTODY

Joint legal custody means that parents "share decision-making
authority as to the important decisions affecting the welfare of the
child." However, when parents cannot agree on those important
decisions, it is appropriate to award sole legal custody to one parent.
A sole legal custodian does not need input or permission from the

other parent to make medical decisions or choose a school for the child. Legal custody also impacts a parent's ability to change the child's domicile (discussed in chapter 5). Before changing legal custody, the parent must demonstrate that the legal custodial issues pass the *Vodvarka* threshold (discussed in chapter 3).

PROBLEM AREAS IN LEGAL CUSTODY DECISIONS

EVALUATING THE BEST INTERESTS OF THE CHILD.

Oftentimes trial judges are asked to modify both physical and legal custody. In those situations, trial judges frequently lump together their analysis on both issues. However, it is not appropriate for trial judges to go through all the best interest factors for physical custody and then just throw in legal custody as an afterthought. The two queries are different, and trial judges should independently consider each question.

Some trial judges do not go through the best-interest analysis for legal custody, even when that is the only question before the court. In *Butler v Simmons-Butler*, the relationship between the mother and father deteriorated quickly after they married. The parties accused each other of domestic abuse, and the mother accused the father of inappropriate behavior toward one of the children. Throughout the turmoil of litigation, the parents underwent counseling and filed various motions. The mother was even held in contempt of court and incarcerated for not returning the children after parenting time. The judge awarded the father sole legal and physical custody.

Although the Court of Appeals's decision in *Butler* discussed legal and physical custody separately, on the legal custody issue, the Court merely said "[t]hrough her behavior, [the mother] has demonstrated that she is both unwilling and unable to communicate and cooperate with [the father] in a manner that is in the children's best interests" and then indicated that the trial judge's detailed best-interest findings related to physical custody were sufficient. However, those findings did not reveal any facts relating to a legal custodial issue—medical, school, or religion.

The trial judge's reasoning on legal custody was even more scant in *Eckdahl v Eckdahl*. The father, who had returned from military deployment in Korea, sought sole legal and physical custody. The trial judge granted both, and the mother appealed. On the legal custody issue, the Court of Appeals held that a remand was necessary because "the circuit court failed to explain on the record why the defendant should be granted sole legal custody." Although the trial judge considered all the best-interest factors, "its analysis primarily related to physical custody, not legal custody. The trial judge did not make any findings regarding whether the parties can and will cooperate and agree on important decisions affecting the welfare of the child ... and the failure to do so requires a remand." Therefore, the Court of Appeals sent the case back to the trial judge to explain "why a grant of sole legal custody to the father was in the best interest of the child, if that remains the court's conclusion."

KATHY'S STORY:
Multiple Appeals Wear Down Mother

Kathy was a disabled attorney, but she retained sole physical and legal custody of her son after the divorce. Within days of the judgment being entered, the father began to file motions to show cause for custody of Kathy. After seven months of the father's motions on parenting time and custody, including a motion based on the child's absences from school, the trial judge eventually found there was a change of circumstances. The judge completely switched custody to the father. The Court of Appeals held that these absences were not a change from the family's behavior during the marriage. On remand, Kathy asked the judge to consider up-to-date evidence on how her son was doing. The judge refused. Sadly, the Court of Appeals also ignored the law and kept the remanded custody order in place.

The trial judge's decision had a long-term impact on this family, especially the child. Kathy described her son as a good kid who, more than anything, wanted to make his father happy. She felt the trial judge did not listen to or respect her and wanted her to just do what her ex-husband told her. The decision also drastically affected her relationship with her son. Before the custody ruling, she had been the one to bring him up, but the court decision "still affects him to this day because he has spent most of his high school days with his father and not his mother." She says he "was so innocent in all of this, and it was wrong to put him in a tug-of-war situation." Ultimately, Kathy decided to stop arguing with her ex-husband because it only hurt her son more, and it had already taken "an emotional toll on him not to have both parents present" in his life.

WHEN LEGAL CUSTODY PROBLEMS BLEED INTO PHYSICAL CUSTODY AND PARENTING-TIME DECISIONS

The Child Custody Act is not clear on the distinction between physical and legal custody, so it is no wonder trial judges often intermingle the issues. In *Gusmano v Gusmano* (see "Kathy's Story"), the father filed a motion for sole legal and physical custody because their son was frequently absent from school. The trial judge granted the motion. That decision was eventually upheld by the Court of Appeals. Even though a legal custodial issue—the child's schooling—was the impetus for the modification motion, that issue resulted in the child switching schedules so that he was primarily with his father and spent alternating weekends with his mother.

A disagreement between the parents about important decisions usually should not alter the character or amount of the time each parent spends with their child. However, sometimes a change in physical custody is necessary when one parent is awarded sole legal custody. For example, if the parents live far apart and cannot agree on medical

A disagreement between the parents about important decisions usually should not alter the character or amount of the time each parent spends with their child.

decisions, the child might need to live with the parent who is better able to manage the child's medical situation. Along with the award of sole legal custody, the trial judge might have to change parenting time so the child spends more time with the parent in charge of medical decisions. But if the parents live close to each other, there should not be a reason to change parenting time simply because the trial judge awards one parent sole legal custody.

UNRESOLVED ISSUES IN LEGAL CUSTODY CASES

ROUTINE DECISION-MAKING VERSUS "IMPORTANT DECISIONS" AFFECTING THE CHILD'S HEALTH, SAFETY, AND WELFARE

The appellate courts need to address whether disagreements about routine decision-making justify a change of legal custody—they should not. The Child Custody Act and the Michigan Parenting Time Guidelines both recognize a parent's authority to make routine decisions concerning a child, independent of the other parent. The Parenting Time Guidelines state, "If the child(ren) requires medical attention during parenting time, the noncustodial parent should obtain treatment for the child(ren) and notify the custodial parent as soon as possible." The authority to make routine medical decisions is not dependent upon the parent's legal custody status. It arises from exercising parenting time with the child.

Routine decision-making is not the same as making important decisions that affect the child's life. Yet Michigan law does not define "routine" or "important" decisions in custody disputes. What qualifies as routine decision-making? What a child eats or wears in a parent's home surely are routine decisions. What time they go to bed and what friends they play with also seem routine. But what about routine decisions that connect to education, medical, and religious decisions? How a parent handles the child's homework is routine (as long as it is getting done). Whether a child undergoes a risky surgery or is placed on drugs with long-term health consequences is clearly an important decision. But is giving a child an over-the-counter pain reliever a routine or important decision? Whether a child is baptized or what religious faith the child practices is important. But is the child's church attendance during parenting time routine? It would be helpful for an appellate court to provide guidance on the line between routine and important decision-making that impacts the child's welfare.

In *Siesel v Poutney*, the mother had sole legal custody. The parents did not agree on their child's use of a cell phone, and the father purchased a phone for the child without the mother's permission. Based on the cell phone and other issues, the father filed a motion for joint legal custody. Both the referee and the trial judge determined that the father had not met the threshold of proper cause or change in circumstance to modify legal custody. The Court of Appeals affirmed the lower court, saying,

> Decisions regarding the children's use of phones, electronic devices, or social media while at [the mother]'s residence pertain to routine matters left to [her] discretion while the children are in her physical custody. The evidence related to [the mother's] decisions regarding such conduct in [her] home neither establish that the children's well-being has been significantly impacted nor that material changes have had or will almost certainly have an effect on them.

> **PRACTICE TIP:** *Craft your motions to modify legal custody by explaining how the sole legal custodian's decisions are negatively impacting the child's welfare; they are not just important decisions but also have a significant impact on the child. Conversely, in responding to a motion to change legal custody, frame your client's decision in terms of how it is a routine decision and does not significantly impact the welfare of the child.*

"IMPORTANT DECISIONS" AFFECTING THE HEALTH, SAFETY, AND WELFARE OF THE CHILD

Parents and trial judges need a framework for determining which decisions are important enough to require court intervention and which are routine and left to the parent exercising parenting time. The trial judge should not be involved in routine decisions, beyond advising the parties that such decisions are within the sole authority of the parent exercising parenting time. However, in *Bauer v Waedelich*, the Court of Appeals rejected the father's argument that "treatment of the children's allergies, ear infections, and related illnesses are routine matters." Instead, the trial judge awarded the mother sole legal custody due to the parties' inability to get along on medical decisions, including very routine decisions like the administration of over-the-counter medicine or taking the child to an after-hours medical facility.

If one parent disagrees with the other parent's routine decisions, then the only way for the trial judge to impinge on that decision-making would be by placing restrictions on that parent's time. Under the Child Custody Act, parenting time can be restricted if the parent shows by "clear and convincing evidence that it would endanger the child's physical, mental, or emotional health." But the list of restrictions that a trial judge can place on a parent's time is intended to "facilitate the orderly and meaningful exercise of parenting time by a parent," not impinge on routine decision-making. It includes things like transportation, the presence of third parties, and supervision. The Act also includes the ability of the trial judge to impose "[a]ny other reasonable condition determined to be appropriate in the particular case." Presumably, this catch-all factor could encompass some routine decision-making. What that looks like, apparently, is left to the imagination of the parties and trial judges, as there are no cases exploring this issue.

WHEN THE PARENTS CANNOT AGREE ON THE CHILD'S EXTRACURRICULAR ACTIVITIES

Is the child's involvement in extracurricular activities a routine decision? What if that activity infringes on the other parent's time with the child? This is a frequently occurring issue without clear guidance, so attorneys and parties plow ahead on a case-by-case basis. All activities are not created equal. A child taking a short-term cooking class is not the same as engaging in a travel soccer league. Being on the high school football team (with daily practice and Friday-night games) is not the same as a child who participates in Scouts after school twice per month. At least one Court of Appeals decision has analyzed extracurricular activities in the context of legal custody. In *Stanley v Thompson*, the parents could not agree on nearly any decision affecting the child's welfare. They disagreed over flu shots, extracurricular activities, school enrollment, and child therapy. Even when the parents eventually agreed on these decisions, their delay affected the well-being of the children. To solve this problem, the trial judge ultimately awarded one parent sole legal custody.

Other cases appear to include extracurriculars with parenting time or physical custody. In *Shade v Wright*, the trial judge modified parenting time to accommodate the child's sports activities. The father, whose parenting time was reduced by the order, appealed. The Court of Appeals affirmed the modification of parenting time because the child was now in high school, and the modification served the child's best interests.

INTERVIEWING THE CHILD FOR REASONABLE PREFERENCE IN A LEGAL CUSTODY DISPUTE

While there are many appellate decisions about a child's reasonable preference, those cases invariably discuss who the child prefers to live with. But legal custody is another important aspect of the trial judge's custody decision. Arguably, legal custody plays as significant a role in a child's life as physical custody. Legal custody has huge psychological and physical implications for a child's custodial environment. Changes in the legal custody arrangement can affect a child's major healthcare decisions and which school and church the child attends. A child is just as likely to have a reasonable preference on legal custody issues as on the overnights in each parent's home (see "Jenna's Story").

JENNA'S STORY:
Child Is Forced to Stay in a County Where Neither Parent Wants to Live

Jenna and her daughter lived in Howell for years. After the divorce, her ex-husband moved to Oakland and then Wayne County. Jenna remarried a man who worked in Berrien County. As no parent lived or wanted to live in Livingston County, Jenna filed a motion to change her daughter's school to Berrien County, and the father filed a motion to change custody. The judge denied the father's custody motion, keeping his weekend parenting time. But the judge also ordered the child to stay in the Howell schools. Jenna and her husband were having a baby, but due to the judge's order, Jenna could not live with her husband. The decision tore the family apart once again. The Court of Appeals said that the husband could change jobs to be within one hundred miles of Howell, and then Jenna could move with her daughter.

The judge's ruling has made things worse. Because the child told the court that she preferred to stay in her current school—and the trial judge let her—the child now thinks she is the boss. Jenna felt the judge was clueless about what was happening in her case and failed to find out what was really going on. The judge also seemed completely insensitive to the untenable situation the judge's decision has put her family in, which will only get more difficult as time goes by.

There are no published decisions that address the child's preference when it comes to legal custodial decisions. But hypothetically, the trial judge should be able to ask the child which school they prefer to attend, which parent they want to bring them to the doctor, or which church they prefer. All these questions will give the judge information about the child's preference as it pertains to legal custodial decisions. According to *Kubicki v Sharp,* when the trial judge fails to interview the children or determine if they are capable of expressing a reasonable preference on physical custody, the appellate court "must vacate the circuit court's order and remand for a new custody hearing." Why should the result be any different when it comes to the important decisions controlling a child's life?

BEST INTERESTS RELATED TO LEGAL CUSTODY

Not all the best-interest factors relate to legal custody decisions, so the analysis for legal custody is or should be somewhat different than for physical custody. For instance, how does the permanence of the family unit (factor e), the love and affection shared between the child and parent (factor a), or stability and permanence of the residence (factor d) relate to important decisions like medical treatment and education? They probably do not. But other best-interest factors are more strongly associated with legal custody decisions, such as the capacity and disposition of the parent to provide the child with medical and other remedial care (factor c) or the capacity and disposition of the parent to "continue the education and raising of the child in his or her religion or creed" (factor b). The appellate courts should issue a binding decision outlining the process for trial courts to determine how the best interest factors apply to that analysis.

KEY TAKEAWAYS

- Legal custody ensures that each parent is involved in <u>important decisions</u> that affect a child's life, including <u>medical, educational, and religious decisions.</u>

- When parents cannot agree on important decisions, the judge may award <u>sole legal custody</u> to one parent, but the noncustodial parent is still entitled to access medical and educational information.

- The Child Custody Act provides vague distinctions between physical and legal custody, which leads to trial court errors.

- The authority of each parent to make <u>routine decisions</u> concerning a child is recognized by Michigan law—although it does not distinguish between "routine" and "important" decisions, and the Court of Appeals has yet to directly address the issue.

RESOURCES FOR CHAPTER FOUR

LEGAL CUSTODY AND THE LAW

Butler v Simmons-Butler, 308 Mich App 195; 863 NW2d 677 (2014).

Dailey v Kloenhamer, 291 Mich App 660; 811 NW2d 501 (2011).

Eckdahl v Eckdahl, unpublished per curiam opinion of Court of Appeals, issued September 22, 2011 (Docket No. 302029).

Stanley v Thompson, unpublished per curiam opinion of Court of Appeals, issued March 17, 2020 (Docket No. 349779).

Lombardo v Lombardo, 202 Mich App 151; 507 NW2d 788 (1993).

ROUTINE VERSUS IMPORTANT DECISIONS

State Court Administrative Office, *Michigan Parenting Time Guideline* <https://courts.michigan.gov/Administration/SCAO/

OfficesPrograms/FOC/Documents/pt_gdlns.pdf> (accessed June 11, 2021).

Bauer v Waidelich, unpublished per curiam opinion of Court of Appeals, issued August 6, 2019 (Docket No. 345756).

Siesel v Pountney, unpublished per curiam opinion of Court of Appeals, issued June 18, 2019 (Docket No. 346930).

MCL 722.26(a).

MCL 722.26(a)(4).

MCL 722.27(a)(7).

MCL 722.27(a)(11).

CHAPTER FIVE

DOMICILE

When One Parent Wants to Move Far Away

THE PURPOSE OF DOMICILE LAW

Change of domicile law focuses on the effect a move has on a child and their relationships with their parents. Generally, the child should be able to move with a parent who has established a custodial environment. But if the child has an established custodial environment with both parents, judges should be cautious in disrupting those environments unless it has compelling reasons to do so.

QUICK LEGAL SUMMARY OF CHANGE OF DOMICILE

The Court of Appeals laid out the steps a trial judge must go through in analyzing a change of domicile request in *Rains v Rains*. First, the parent who wants to move the child must file a motion, and the trial judge must consider the following:

1. Does the move have "the capacity to improve the quality of life for the child and the relocating parent"?

2. Have both parents followed court orders, and does the relocating parent want to move "to frustrate the other parent's parenting time"?

3. Can both parents remain involved in the child's life and "preserve the parent-child relationship"?

4. Is the parent opposing the move doing so to avoid increased child support?

5. Is "domestic violence part of the reason why the relocating parent wants to move"?

If the parent proves these change-of-domicile factors by a preponderance of the evidence, then the trial judge must ask whether the move would change the child's **established custodial environment**. If not, then the trial judge can allow the move without any further inquiry. If, however, the move will change the child's established custodial environment, then the trial judge must decide if there is clear and convincing evidence that the move is in the child's best interest using the factors in the Child Custody Act.

If the child has an established custodial environment with both parents, judges should be cautious in disrupting those environments unless it has compelling reasons to do so.

There are several significant circumstances where a parent can avoid an evidentiary hearing to change domicile:

1. The other parent consents to the move.

2. The relocating parent has sole legal custody.

3. The move brings the parents' residences closer together.

4. The parents lived more than one hundred miles apart at the time of the original judgment.

PROBLEM AREAS IN CHANGE OF DOMICILE DECISIONS

THE PARENT HAS ALREADY MOVED WHEN THE DOMICILE MOTION IS DENIED

Domicile cases demonstrate how the trial judge's delay in deciding a motion can itself be disruptive to the family. Most times, a parent will not file a motion to change domicile until they have obtained a job offer that requires them to relocate. But once that job offer comes in, the opportunity does not stay open indefinitely. This puts the relocating parent in the unenviable position of having to accept a job offer and move, without knowing whether the trial judge will allow the child to move with them, or hope that the company will keep the job offer open until the trial judge makes a decision. In counties where the trial judges refer domicile motions to the Friend of the Court (FOC) for an initial recommendation, that process can delay the ultimate decision. It is not unusual for domicile motions to take more than six months from the time of filing until a decision.

When the custodial parent has already made the decision to accept a job offer and move more than one hundred miles away, there is the potential that denying the parent's request to change the child's domicile will also change the child's established custodial environment. This has come up in several cases such as *Yachcik v Yachcik,* where the trial judge did not think the moving parent proved the domicile factors by a preponderance of the evidence but did not analyze whether denying the domicile request would actually result in a change of custody. The Court of Appeals reversed the trial judge's decision and remanded for a decision on whether there was clear and convincing evidence that keeping the child in Michigan with the nonrelocating parent was in the child's best interests.

TRIAL JUDGES MUST STILL DECIDE BEST INTEREST WHEN THE MOVING PARENT HAS SOLE LEGAL CUSTODY

A parent with sole legal custody does not have to go through the steps of proving the change of domicile factors by a preponderance of the evidence. However, the Court of Appeals held in *Sulaica v Rometty* that if that move will change the established custodial environment, the trial judge must still hold an evidentiary hearing to ensure that the best interests of the child are proven by clear and convincing evidence.

ADDING UP MILES ON SUCCESSIVE MOVES

There have been instances where a parent moved multiple times, but each individual move was never over the one hundred-mile limit. The Court of Appeals has instructed trial judges to measure the miles between the new proposed home and the residence at the time of the judgment of divorce. If the distance totals more than one hundred miles, then the relocating parent needs to go through the domicile hearing to change the child's residence. Thus, the one hundred-mile rule applies not to the incremental moves—each one less than one hundred miles—but the total mileage between the new home and the residence at the time of the original judgment.

MEASURING MILES AS THE CROW FLIES

The Court of Appeals instructed trial judges on how to measure miles in change of domicile cases. In *Bowers v Vandermeulen-Bowers*, the father sought to change the child's residence from Big Rapids to Byron. Using radial miles (sometimes called "as the crow flies"), the move was ninety-seven miles; whereas using road miles, the move was more than one hundred miles. The mother asserted that the distance should be measured in road miles—based on how many miles the parent and child would have to travel along the road to reach the new residence. She argued that this interpretation of the one hundred-mile rule was consistent with the Child Custody Act's purpose, avoiding disruptions to the child's life caused by parents living more than one hundred miles apart. The trial judge used radial miles, measuring the distance on the map using a straight line. The Court of Appeals agreed with the trial judge's interpretation and held that radial miles was the appropriate method to measure distance in a change of domicile case. The Court's conclusion relied on a case involving the collective bargaining agreements of public employees who were required to live within twenty miles of the nearest boundary of the public employer. The Court of Appeals did not give any credence to the mother's disruption-based argument in favor of road miles, but instead said she should have presented evidence that the father's map was somehow inaccurate.

While the *Bowers* case is binding on the lower courts, its analysis is inconsistent with the Child Custody Act. However, it will take either a contrary Supreme Court decision or a legislative action to overturn the *Bowers* radial-mile rule. Measuring one hundred miles based on a ruler on a map has no correlation with the purpose of the Act or the impact on the child traveling between the two residences. Case in point: A move from Traverse City to Escanaba is ninety-nine radial miles. Under *Bowers*, the trial judge does not have to scrutinize the domicile factors before allowing the parent to move to Escanaba. However, on the ground, the trip takes 263 miles, or 4½ hours, to drive between the two homes. It is hard to see how such a distance does not impact the child in a way that should *at least* require the relocating parent to prove the domicile factors by a preponderance of the evidence. If the parents agreed to meet in the middle for parenting-time exchanges, that location would be Mackinaw City or St. Ignace—certainly not in the middle of Lake Michigan, as the radial miles measurement would suggest. The distance between the homes in road miles could well impact the child's established custodial environment. If both parents shared parenting time and were involved with the child's school activities, the move from Traverse City to Escanaba would most certainly convert an everyday parent into a weekend-only parent. With a travel time of four and a half hours, even alternating weekends might be difficult. With parents meeting in the middle, the child still must spend a significant amount of the weekend traveling in a car—typically Friday evening and then Sunday afternoon, leaving less time for that child to spend with the parent in their Traverse City home.

When a trial judge does not follow the law, it does an injustice to the entire family. It makes fragile and temperamental relationships even worse, which ultimately affects the child in a negative way. Depending on the degree of improper application of the law, the judge also creates an endlessly abusive dynamic where one person (one of the parents or the child) has all the control for the remainder of the child's minority and uses that control to manipulate the other two persons for their desired results in any given situation. A parent that is given control uses it as a threat and a taunt during any disagreement because of the decision that makes that parent "the winner." Or worse, the child plays each parent against the other or takes advantage of a disagreement between the parents for their own personal gain because the court has made the child the decision maker. I have seen this happen in both major custody and minor parenting-time modification cases. The effect on the family far outlives the trial court's jurisdiction and is truly a sad situation to observe.

—**TARA PEARSON**, attorney, Howell, MI

PRACTICE TIP: *If faced with a similar case representing the nonmoving parent, you might file a motion to modify parenting time based on the effect the move had on the feasibility of the existing parenting-time order. This would allow you to address how the move has impacted the best-interest factors. If the case goes to appeal, the appellate attorney can challenge the "as the crow flies" ruling.*

WHEN SUCCESSIVE MOVES CREATE MORE DISTANCE BETWEEN THE PARTIES

Sometimes a parent keeps moving around, such as when that parent or their spouse is in the military. In *Evans v Evans*, the mother had originally obtained permission to move from northern Michigan to Kentucky, where her new husband was stationed in the military. The next move, to Alabama, took the two parents' residences even farther apart, but the mother moved without seeking court permission. Then when her husband was stationed in South Korea, the mother returned to northern Michigan to be close to her family, bringing the children close to their father. The father filed a motion to change custody to keep the children in northern Michigan, anticipating that the mother would move out of state again once her husband returned from South Korea. The Court of Appeals noted its prior decision of *Selhke v Vandermaas*, finding that by moving more than one hundred miles to Alabama without the court's permission, the mother created a change of circumstances to review custody. The Court thus reversed the trial judge's decision to deny the father's custody motion and remanded the case for an evidentiary hearing on whether the change of custody was in the children's best interests.

While the first appeal in *Evans* was pending, the mother planned to move the children to Texas, where her husband was stationed, once again without the court's permission. To prevent that move from happening—particularly while waiting for a decision on the first appeal—the father filed a motion to maintain the status quo of the children living in Michigan. The trial judge denied the father's motion without addressing the domicile factors, ostensibly giving the mother his blessing to move to Texas without a motion. The Court of Appeals determined that the second appeal was moot, based on its recent decision in the first appeal. However, the Court remanded the case and instructed the judge to either grant the father's change of custody motion, keeping the children with him in Michigan, or hold an evidentiary hearing on the mother's change of domicile to Texas according to the Child Custody Act and *Rains*.

WHEN A PARENT'S MOVE IS LESS THAN ONE HUNDRED MILES, BUT OUT OF STATE

Michigan shares borders with three other states, and Canada is only a bridge away in three places. This means that moves can be far less than one hundred miles, yet still be out of state or out of country. The Court of Appeals in *Gagnon v Glowacki* held that a parent is required to obtain court permission to move out of state, even if the move is only a short distance from the child's Michigan residence. The *Gagnon* Court explained that "regardless of the distance involved, if the proposed residence change involves leaving the state, then the factors under MCL 722.31(4) are the proper criteria for the court to consider."

For example, a parent moving from Niles, Michigan, to South Bend, Indiana, only travels eleven miles. Such a short move would not impact the child's established custodial environment. So why does the Child Custody Act make it more difficult to move out of state? It is possible that the Child Custody Act's barrier against out-of-state moves is intended to make it easier to enforce Michigan judgments. An out-of-state move might eventually impact the court's home-state jurisdiction over the child. If a parent obtains permission to move, the Michigan court will retain jurisdiction to modify and enforce its orders as long as one parent lives here.

UNRESOLVED ISSUES IN DOMICILE CASES

FINDINGS ON EACH OF THE DOMICILE FACTORS

Trial judges frequently do not consider all the domicile factors even when they might be relevant to a particular case. Many times, the most important factor before the trial judge is the first one: whether the move has the capacity to improve the lives of the child and the parent. However, the other factors are often relevant as well. In the published opinion of *Yachcik v Yachcik*, the Court of Appeals held that findings on each domicile factor were not required. The *Yachcik* Court reasoned that a finding on each factor was not required because the language in the domicile provision was different than the language of the best-interest provision. The best-interest provision states the best interests of the child are the "sum total of the following factors to be considered, evaluated, and determined by the court," while the domicile provision states, "Before permitting a legal residence change otherwise restricted by subsection (1), the court shall consider each of the following factors, with the child as the primary focus in the court's deliberations."

Even though the domicile provision requires the trial judge to consider each factor, the Court of Appeals instead focused on the word "consider" and contrasted it to the best-interest provision, which instructed that the factors are to be "considered, evaluated, and determined" by the trial judge. Based on a dictionary definition of the term "consider," the Court determined "it is apparent that MCL 722.31(4) requires a trial court to carefully think about, take into account, or assess each factor, but there is no indication that a trial court is required to take further action, such as making explicit findings on the record."

The Court of Appeals's analysis in *Yachcik* was wrong because it completely disregarded the requirement that judges consider each factor—apparently the trial judge only has to think about the factors but not make findings. Not only is the Court of Appeals's decision incongruous with the statutory language, but it allows trial judges to do less work even when the evidence in the record demonstrated that the factor was relevant to the case. If "considering" allows the judge to simply think about the factors without making any factual findings, then there is no record of how the trial judge decided whether to approve the move. This alone seems contrary to the purpose and structure of the Child Custody Act. This interpretation was adopted by the Michigan Supreme Court in *Pierron v Pierron*. Nonetheless, this analysis is troubling and should be challenged in another case or in the Legislature.

THE SOLE LEGAL CUSTODIAN WANTS
TO MOVE OUT OF STATE

Neither the domicile provision nor case law provides authority for what a sole legal custodian must do to obtain permission to move out of state, or what the trial judge can and cannot do in answering that request. The statute is clear that the one hundred-mile rule does not apply if a parent has sole legal custody. Although not mentioned in the domicile provision, the court rules require a parent—even one with sole legal custody—to obtain court permission to move out of state, saying, "the domicile or residence of the minor may not be moved from Michigan without the approval of the judge who awarded custody or the judge's successor." Can a judge impose additional requirements on a sole legal custodian if the move happens to be out of state?

The Court of Appeals in *Brausch v Brausch* held that the court rules and domicile provision do not conflict. The mother wanted to move from Michigan to Canada. The *Brausch* Court reasoned that the parent with sole legal custody "must first obtain the trial court's approval" before moving out of state, but that the factors in the domicile provision "do not apply to the request." The Court of Appeals did not expound on how a sole legal custodian would go about obtaining that approval or what the trial judge was required to consider before approving that request. Curiously, though, the Court said that the trial judge "tacitly approved" the move by denying the father's ex parte request for the child to be returned to Michigan.

The Court of Appeals gave some guidance in *Spires v Bergman*, where a sole legal custodian wanted to change the child's domicile to Texas. It held that the mother's ability to change the child's domicile was not restricted by statute. Thus, once the trial judge determined that it was not required to consider the domicile factors, it properly approved the mother's proposed move. The Court of Appeals held that the trial judge fully satisfied the court rules by first conducting all necessary inquiries under the Act, and that the trial judge did not abuse its discretion by approving the proposed out-of-state move. It seems from the *Spires* case that as long as the court verifies the parties' compliance with or exemption from the domicile statute, then the trial judge can approve or deny a motion for change of domicile under the court rules.

The question remains how trial judges should analyze these domicile requests under the court rules. How does the parent go about obtaining permission to move out of state? Does the parent have to file a motion and just get the court to sign off on the move without going through any of the factors or a hearing? Does the parent just need to inform the court that the parent and child are moving? On what grounds can the trial judge deny the request by a parent who is not required to satisfy the domicile statute? The court rule states that "the person awarded custody must promptly notify the FOC in writing when the minor is moved to another address," but is that enough to satisfy the court rule when that move crosses state lines? The Supreme Court should weigh in on these questions.

LALI'S STORY:

Divorced Mom Cannot Find Local Job in Her Field, but Judge Won't Allow Her to Move with Her Child

Lali and her husband moved to the Upper Peninsula for his university job. As a college art professor, Lali's job opportunities were limited, so she stayed home and raised their son. After the divorce, with no family in the state, no job, and no spousal support, Lali had no choice but to embark on a nationwide job search. She landed a university job in upstate New York, but the judge said no to the move. The judge failed to consider how denying the child's move would also change custody: from the child's primary-caretaker mom to his less-involved father. The judge ruled against Lali even though most of the best-interest factors favored her.

The court process left Lali feeling helpless, an outsider (she is a Muslim). The judge believed Lali should be able to find a job in Michigan despite the evidence that she had looked extensively in the state without success. Now Lali travels the twelve hours from New York to Michigan every other week to see her son, and she speaks to him every day. The judge was mad when the Court of Appeals overturned her decision, but it just gave the judge another opportunity to hurt Lali and her son.

Her son was very upset with the new custody arrangement. He cried every day and was very angry because he did not want to leave Lali's side when his weekends with her ended. He also became isolated in school and did not make many friends due to the harm caused by the court's decision.

WHEN NEITHER PARENT CAN DEMONSTRATE CLEAR AND CONVINCING EVIDENCE TO SUPPORT THE CUSTODY CHANGE CREATED BY A CHANGE OF DOMICILE

On some occasions, either granting or denying the move would change the child's established custodial environment with one of their parents. This is because a parent usually seeks to relocate due to remarriage or a new job, but the trial judge's decision is limited to whether the child should move, not the parent. If the parent has already moved, then denying the change of domicile could impact the child's established custodial environment when the child cannot move with the custodial parent. How should the court decide a motion to change domicile when either a grant or denial will work to change the established custodial environment? How does the trial judge decide the combined domicile/custody motion?

In *Cleary v Khalid* (see "Lali's Story"), the mother sought a change of domicile when she was offered a university job in New York, but the trial judge denied the request. The trial judge found that the child had an established custodial environment with both parents and then considered the father's change-of-custody motion. In doing so, the trial judge failed to consider several of the best-interest factors. On appeal, the mother argued that the proposed parenting-time schedule allowed the child to retain a joint established custodial environment with both parents. The Court of Appeals disagreed, concluding that either parent needed to establish change of custody by clear and convincing evidence. Because denying the mother's motion to change domicile—when she had already accepted the job in Ithaca and moved to New York—was a change in the child's established custodial environment, the Court of Appeals held that the father establishing that custody with him was in the child's best interest by clear and convincing evidence.

In *Eads v Scott* (see "Wally's Story"), the parents shared equal parenting even after the mother moved nearly two hundred miles away. But once it was time for kindergarten, fifty-fifty parenting time was not possible. The mother filed a motion to change domicile to her new residence. The trial judge found that the mother satisfied the domicile factors and then found that the child had an established custodial environment with both parents. Turning to the best-interest factors, the trial judge commented that the facts were "very close" and basically found the parents equal, giving the mother the slightest edge on a couple of factors. The Court of Appeals reversed the trial judge for not following the framework of *Rains v Rains*. Specifically, the trial judge looked at whether the change of custody was warranted under the best-interest factors, but it should have looked at whether the change of domicile was in the child's best interest. On remand, even though the trial judge made multiple errors, the Court of Appeals affirmed the trial judge's decision to award custody to the mother.

WALLY'S STORY:
Mother Moves without Court Permission, yet Father Ends Up with the Short End of the Arrangement

After their divorce, Wally and his ex-wife lived close to each other and maintained daily contact with their young son. But the mom remarried and moved nearly two hundred miles away without court permission. The trial judge allowed the mom to keep custody of the son while the case was going on and eventually awarded the mom custody, making it so Wally's son could only see his father and half siblings on alternating weekends.

Wally was very upset that the mom was rewarded for violating court orders–"The order is there for a reason!" The mom also made things difficult by requiring Wally to pick up his son from a distance of two hundred miles away, even though she made frequent trips back "home" to see her family.

Wally feels that his son gets "lost in the mix" with the half siblings and stepsiblings at his mother's home. The child was always excited to see Wally, giving him a big hug and telling him how much he loves him. The two talk on the phone daily, and his son texts him "Good morning" every day when he wakes up. Wally expressed that the court did not understand or consider his son's feelings when making the decision. By keeping the mom's new family together, the judge broke up Wally's family. Wally believes the family court system is deeply flawed, and he hopes that changes are made to correct those flaws. All Wally wants is to have a strong relationship with his son.

KEY TAKEAWAYS

- If a child has an established custodial environment with both parents, then the court should be cautious about disrupting that environment with a move *unless* there is a compelling reason.

- The one hundred-mile rule applies to the total mileage as measured in radial miles, from the latest move to the residence at the time of the judgment of divorce, and not to incremental moves, even if each was less than one hundred miles.

- Neither the domicile provision nor case law provides guidance for how a sole legal custodian goes about obtaining permission to move out of state.

RESOURCES FOR CHAPTER FIVE

JUDICIAL ERRORS

Brausch v Brausch, 283 Mich App 339; 770 NW2d 77 (2009).

Cleary v Khalid, unpublished per curiam opinion of Court of Appeals, issued May 28, 2019 (Docket No. 345719).

Eads v Scott, unpublished per curiam opinion of Court of Appeals, issued February 28, 2017 (Docket No. 333949).

Evans v Evans, unpublished per curiam opinion of Court of Appeals, issued February 20, 2015 (Docket No. 323126).

Sehlke v Vandermaas, 268 Mich App 262; 707 NW2d 603 (2005).

DOMICILE STANDARDS

Gagnon v Glowacki, 295 Mich App 557; 815 NW2d 141 (2012).

Rains v Rains, 301 Mich App 313; 836 NW2d 709 (2013).

Rittershaus v Rittershaus, 273 Mich App 462; 730 NW2d 262 (2007).

Spires v Bergman, 276 Mich App 432; 741 NW2d 523 (2007).

Sulaica v Rometty, 308 Mich App 568; 866 NW2d 838 (2014).

MCR 3.211.

MCL 722.31.

MEASURING MILES OF MOVES

Bowers v Vandermeulen-Bowers, 278 Mich App 287; 750 NW2d 597 (2008).

Eickelberg v Eickelberg, 309 Mich App 694; 871 NW2d 561 (2015).

CHAPTER SIX

PARENTING TIME

Hurdles to Obtaining More
Time with Your Kids

THE PURPOSE OF PARENTING TIME

The Child Custody Act acknowledges that it is "in the best interests of a child for the child to have a strong relationship with both of his or her parents." Trial judges must award parenting time "in a frequency, duration, and type reasonably calculated to promote a strong relationship between the child and the parent." Depriving a child of a parent is a drastic measure that should only be undertaken under dire circumstances, and then using the Act's procedures.

QUICK LEGAL SUMMARY OF PARENTING TIME

The Child Custody Act's parenting-time provisions address several factors trial judges must consider when awarding parenting time. A parent should not be denied parenting time unless "it is shown on the record by clear and convincing evidence that it would endanger the child's physical, mental, or emotional health." In addition to the best-interest factors (discussed in chapters 2 and 3), the trial judge should also consider the parenting-time factors listed in the statute, including special circumstances of the child, whether the child is nursing, the likelihood of abuse or neglect during parenting time, and so on.

The threshold to modify parenting time is lower than the threshold to modify custody. Under *Shade v Wright*, normal life changes, such as a child moving from elementary to middle school, can trigger a parenting-time modification. So can the parent's work schedule, the child's extracurricular activities, and any number of factors that would not be enough to reexamine custody.

There's an even lower threshold to modify a condition on parenting time, such as drug testing, limits on third persons, supervision requirements, or other restrictions imposed on a parent's conduct during their parenting time. Because changes to these conditions will generally not affect an established custodial environment or the frequency or duration of parenting time, the Court of Appeals in *Kaeb v Kaeb* explained it was "persuaded that a lesser, more flexible understanding of 'proper cause' or 'change in circumstances' should apply." Due to this lower threshold, "the party requesting a change to an existing condition on the exercise of parenting time must demonstrate proper cause or a change in circumstances that would justify a trial judge's determination that the condition in its current form no longer serves the child's best interests."

PROBLEM AREAS IN PARENTING-TIME DECISIONS

CALLING IT "PARENTING TIME"
RESULTS IN WRONG THRESHOLD

When a parenting-time modification impacts the established custodial environment, then the modification must be treated as a custody motion using the clear and convincing standard. Many trial judges apply the wrong standard to the threshold question, just like in *Lieberman* (discussed in chapter 3). This often results in a parent's parenting-time motion being denied for failing to satisfy the higher *Vodvarka* custody threshold. Conversely, trial judges may also hold evidentiary hearings on parents' motions even though their allegations don't reach the parenting-time threshold. As a result, trial judges may apply the wrong **burden of proof** when it analyzes the best interests of the child.

> **Practice Tip:** *Help the trial judge apply the correct threshold standard by including it in your briefs and arguments. Whether trial counsel represents the moving parent or the parent opposing modification, applying the wrong evidentiary standard could harm your client and the children if the case must be appealed later to correct the legal error.*

EVALUATING BEST INTERESTS FOR A
PARENTING-TIME MODIFICATION

The Act's parenting-time provision says that parenting time should be awarded based on the best interests of the child. Any time a trial judge makes a parenting-time decision, the judge should consider the relevant best-interest factors. The Michigan Supreme Court's decision in *Pierron v Pierron* and the Court of Appeals in *Shade v Wright* both confirm that the statutory best-interest factors are relevant to parenting-time decisions. *Shade* further elaborated that "custody decisions require findings under all of the best-interest factors, but parenting-time decisions may be made with findings on only the contested issues." Some courts have failed to do this, thinking that a parenting-time modification does not require a thorough best-interest analysis. However, in *Ludwig v Ludwig*, the Supreme Court held that to modify parenting time, the trial judge must first hold an evidentiary hearing and consider the best interests of the children.

> *Any time a trial judge makes a parenting-time decision, the judge should consider the relevant best-interest factors.*

PARENTING-TIME ORDERS ARE NOT APPEALABLE BY RIGHT

Parenting time modification orders are not appealable by right. As discussed in chapter 1, since January 1, 2019, the court rule limits an appeal by right to postjudgment orders granting or denying a change of physical custody, legal custody, or domicile. Most parenting-time modifications no longer qualify as final orders that parents can appeal by right. The Court of Appeals should look at the substance of the decision and determine whether the trial judge's order changed custody, regardless of the title of the motion filed by one parent.

PRACTICE TIP: *When a change in overnights is needed, consider preserving your client's appeal by right by requesting both a change of custody and a change in parenting time as alternative forms of relief. Even if the court determines you have not met the Vodvarka threshold, the denial of the custody portion of your motion will render the decision a final order for appeal.*

Treating parenting-time orders differently than custody orders on appeal creates several problems. First, custody appeals are expedited, but parenting-time appeals are not. This creates a tremendous delay in obtaining a decision in a case modifying parenting time. The parent must file an application for leave and wait six months or more for the Court of Appeals to grant or deny the application (unless the parent files an emergency motion). If the Court grants leave, the case will proceed on the slow track for non-custody cases, which could drag out for another year. By contrast, the total time in an appeal by right for custody cases is eight to ten months. Delay is bad for families. Giving one parent more parenting time naturally means that time is being taken away from the other parent. Depending on the facts, a trial judge's erroneous parenting-time decision could take the children out of a safe and nurturing environment or leave them in a potentially harmful situation. The longer a parenting-time appeal takes, the longer the children's lives are in flux, and the more time they will potentially spend in a home where they should not be.

Second, when an order purports to modify parenting time but actually changes custody, the appellate courts may not give that decision the proper review. Under the former court rule, these orders were appealable by right as "affecting custody." But now an appeal by right is limited to an order granting or denying a motion to change custody. What happens when the motion only seeks to modify parenting time, but then the trial judge proceeds to change custody? The Court of Appeals should treat such an order as a custody decision, but there is no guarantee it will do so. That leaves families uncertain of their appellate rights and how their cases will proceed on appeal. Like delay, uncertainty is also bad for families. Applying for leave to appeal a parenting-time decision creates more uncertainty because there is no guarantee that the Court of Appeals will grant the application. If it does, the appeal will take longer. And if it doesn't, then the parent is left without a remedy. When leave is denied in a single-sentence order, parents are left without closure or understanding of why the Court of Appeals refused to hear their appeal.

Third, it is unfair to deny families an appeal by right for many parenting-time modifications. While some changes in the parenting-time schedule may not be significant enough to justify an appeal by right (for example, granting a parent two more overnights per month), many times, parenting-time orders represent more significant changes. For example, a parent suddenly increasing from zero to six overnights per month with a young child is a significant change in that child's life. But since the change is merely parenting time, the other parent can only challenge the increase in an application for leave. This is true even though each modification motion is like its own mini-case—based on new facts that did not exist at the time of the last custody order. The trial judge is making a decision on those new facts for the first and only time. Yet that decision is not considered a final order. Without an appeal by right, an unhappy parent has no guarantee the Court of Appeals will ever review the trial judge's decision.

We always encourage our clients to agree to work together for what's right for their family and their children. The parents should ask themselves, "Is this parenting-time decision for the parent or for the child?" It should be about what is in the best interest of the child.

—SUSAN LICHTERMAN, attorney, Jaffe
Raitt Heuer & Weiss, Detroit, MI

UNRESOLVED ISSUES IN PARENTING-TIME CASES

WHEN A PARENTING-TIME CHANGE AMOUNTS TO A CUSTODY MODIFICATION

There is no bright-line rule on how many days in the parenting-time schedule a trial judge can modify before it becomes a custody change. Many cases discuss the number of overnights that would tip the balance from parenting time to custody modification. In *Lieberman*, the trial judge held that "swapping" the parents' schedules (the mother went from 225 to 140 overnights per year) was a mere parenting-time modification. The Court of Appeals disagreed. But few other cases address whether a parenting-time modification changed the child's established custodial environment.

In 2018, the Court of Appeals explained in *Sternaman v Sternaman*:

> In determining whether a proposed change to parenting time would alter an established custodial environment, an important consideration is to what extent the proposed change will decrease a parent's time with the child. Whereas minor modifications that leave a party's parenting time essentially intact do not change a child's established custodial

environment, significant changes do. In other words, a substantial modification of parenting time that significantly reduces the amount of time that a parent with an established custodial environment spends with a child would alter the established custodial environment, and such a proposed change must be considered under *Vodvarka*.

The Court of Appeals held that reducing one parent's overnights by twenty-six to fifty-seven days per year was not a "minor" modification that left the parenting time "essentially intact."

REMOVING A CONDITION ON PARENTING TIME

The father in *Kaeb v Kaeb* had several conditions on his parenting time: he had to continue alcohol treatment, go to therapy, and attend AA meetings. After many months of sobriety, the father filed a motion to remove the conditions. He supported his motion with a psychological evaluation that stated there was "no clinical reason" for him to continue attending AA meetings and a letter from his therapist discharging him from therapy and saying he had benefitted. The trial judge refused to remove these conditions on his parenting time, holding that the father had not shown a "change of circumstances." The trial judge concluded that the father's motion was "without legal basis" and sanctioned him for filing it. A short time later, the trial judge decided "it would 'cancel those two requirements' of its own accord ... [because the father] was plainly determined not to participate and would not benefit from them."

These facts led the Court of Appeals to articulate a new threshold standard to modify a condition on parenting time. The Court of Appeals explained that "ordinary changes in the parties' behavior, status, or living conditions might justify a trial court in finding that a previously imposed condition is no longer in the child's best interests." The Court of Appeals held that "a party establishes proper cause to revisit the condition if he or she demonstrates that there is an appropriate ground for taking legal action."

Yet even after *Kaeb*, many judges still make it unduly burdensome to remove a condition on parenting time. It is unclear what a parent must prove to a trial judge to have a condition on parenting time removed. For example, one mother sought to remove the requirement for supervised parenting time. The trial judge held that allowing unsupervised parenting time would change the established custodial environment. The judge held the mother to the *Vodvarka* standard rather than the less-stringent *Kaeb* standard. The trial judge did not explain how modifying the condition on supervised parenting time would "affect an established custodial environment or alter the frequency or duration of parenting time." He denied the mother's motion on this threshold issue without ever determining whether unsupervised parenting time was in the children's best interests. Even though the trial judge held the mother to the custody standard, the Court of Appeals said it was simply the denial of a parenting-time motion, forcing her to file an application for leave to appeal the decision. Cases like this demonstrate that trial judges, practitioners, and parents need guidance from the Court of Appeals on how to apply the *Kaeb* threshold to alter a condition on parenting time.

THE DIFFICULTY OF PAYING FOR A PARENTING-TIME SUPERVISOR

In *Martin v Martin*, a mother's parenting time had been suspended until she could set up supervised times with a specific supervisor. The mother claimed she could not do so, in part because she could not pay the supervisor's outstanding invoices. The Court of Appeals did not disturb the trial judge's decision requiring supervision, but it expressed concern over how difficult it was for the mother to regain her parenting time:

> Although we affirm the trial court's custody order, we are concerned that [the mother] has been completely unable to visit or communicate with [the child] since the order issued. The court ordered parenting time to be supervised by [the supervisor] and precluded any outside communication unless [the supervisor] determines that it would be in [the child]'s best interests. However, according to [the mother], [the supervisor] has refused to participate in any supervised parenting-time sessions until [the mother] makes payments, which [the mother] claims she cannot afford. If this is true, it is quite troubling as the trial court has already determined that it is in [the child]'s best interests to have a relationship with both parents, and a complete deprivation of contact with either parent is against the child's best interests. Within the last month, the trial court issued orders attempting to alleviate this issue. In the event the problem has not been resolved, [the mother] is free to file a new motion below. If she does, the court must consider the financial impact of its orders and craft any remedy necessary to promote [the child]'s best interests. We highlight that which the trial court so adroitly communicated throughout these challenging proceedings: it is in a child's best interests to have a healthy relationship with *both* parents.

DIFFICULTY IN REINSTATING PARENTING TIME

That a trial judge might put up insurmountable barriers to parenting time is very concerning. An indefinite suspension of parenting time can be almost as bad as having the trial judge terminate parental rights. In *Luna v Regnier*, the mother had been trying for years to reunify with her children. The case started with a CPS petition based on the filthy and unsafe condition of the father's home. The mother was dragged into the case even though the allegations of abuse and neglect did not involve her. Eventually, the father made improvements to his home, and the trial judge closed the CPS case against him but kept the case open against the mother because she had allegedly not been cooperating with CPS (see chapter 12). Her parental rights were terminated until the Michigan Supreme Court vacated that order for due process violations (see chapter 1). The children lived with their father during the lengthy period between the mother's termination trial and the Michigan Supreme Court's order vacating the termination order. Once the Supreme Court's decision finally gave the mother a chance to reunify with her children, the trial judge in the custody case decided that the children (who felt that their mother had abandoned them) should not be forced into parenting time with her until they wanted it. The trial judge suspended the mother's parenting time indefinitely with no mechanism for her to resume a relationship with her children. The Court of Appeals in *Luna* slightly modified the trial judge's decision, instructing the judge to hold regular review hearings to determine whether the children were ready to resume parenting time.

Similarly, in the *O'Brien* case, the trial judge allowed the children to decide whether they were willing to "reinstate contact" as a condition on the mother resuming her parenting time with the children. Judge Gleicher, in her dissenting opinion, commented that "children are

141

not emotionally or intellectually capable of being assigned the role of parenting-time gatekeepers and under no circumstances should be granted this power." The children in *O'Brien* had been estranged from their mother for over two years due to the temporary custody order. Judge Gleicher concluded, "In its haste to punish the mother, the trial court wound up worsening a bad situation."

Ironically, parents in CPS cases have more protections than parents in custody cases. First, a parent in a CPS case has the right to an attorney, including appointed counsel if the parent cannot afford to hire their own. That parent also has the right to an appointed appellate attorney if the case moves to appeal. In contrast, many parents struggle to keep up with the cost of attorney fees in ongoing custody cases. Many attorneys are leery of cases with extensive litigation history or where one parent's parenting time has been suspended, because those cases tend to be time consuming. Firms may not have the resources to take on that type of case for a reduced fee while also representing other paying clients.

Second, in a CPS case, the goal is typically to reunify the parent and the child. By law, the Department of Health and Human Services (DHHS) must make efforts to reunify the parent and child by offering services such as parenting-time classes, individual and family therapy sessions, anger management classes, or drug testing. All these services are paid for by the state of Michigan or the county. In contrast, parents in custody cases are not entitled to any kind of services from the state to help them reunify with their children when parenting time has been restricted.

Third, parents in CPS cases often receive some sort of parenting time. If the judge orders supervised parenting time, the state or county pays for that supervision. In contrast, a parent who is granted supervised parenting time in a custody case will need to find a court-approved supervisor and pay them out of pocket. In *Martin*, the mother's inability to pay the court-approved supervisor prevented her from having any parenting time with her child. If a parent's parenting time is indefinitely suspended in a custody case, they may prefer a CPS case where at least they may have an opportunity to spend time with their child.

KEY TAKEAWAYS

- Applying the <u>wrong threshold standard </u>for a parenting-time modification will lead to other legal errors, so it is important for the trial court to carefully apply the proper legal standard.

- Most parenting-time orders no longer are <u>appealable by right,</u> but appellate courts should not treat parenting-time orders differently than custody orders when the order impacts the quality and character of the child's time with their parent.

- There is no bright-line rule on how many overnights tip the balance from a parenting-time modification to a custody modification, but a <u>substantial modification of parenting time</u> that significantly reduces the amount of time that a parent with an established custodial environment spends with a child affects custody.

- Many trial courts make it unduly burdensome to <u>remove a condition</u> on parenting time, and the Court of Appeals has yet to provide clear guidance on how to remove a condition on parenting time.

RESOURCES FOR CHAPTER SIX

PARENTING-TIME MODIFICATION

Pierron v Pierron, 282 Mich App 222; 765 NW2d 345 (2009).

Shade v Wright, 291 Mich App 17; 805 NW2d 1 (2010).

Sternaman v Sternaman, unpublished per curiam opinion of Court of Appeals, issued July 31, 2018 (Docket No. 340722).

MCL 722.27(a).

CONDITIONS ON PARENTING TIME

Jacob v Jacob, unpublished per curiam opinion of Court of Appeals, issued March 3, 2020 (Docket No. 344580).

Kaeb v Kaeb, 309 Mich App 556; 873 NW2d 319 (2015).

Ludwig v Ludwig, 501 Mich 1075; 911 NW2d 462 (2018).

Martin v Martin, unpublished per curiam opinion of Court of Appeals, issued January 28, 2020 (Docket No. 349261).

ADDITIONAL RESOURCES

Speaker Law Firm, *Tips for Parenting Time Appeals* < https://bit.ly/3gsWnjf> (accessed June 11, 2021).

CHAPTER SEVEN

GRANDPARENTING TIME

The Many Legal Steps to Obtain
Time with Grandchildren

THE PURPOSE OF GRANDPARENTING TIME

Although children frequently benefit from close relationships with their grandparents, that benefit does not overcome a parent's right to make decisions about who their child associates with, including relatives. A fit parent can deny grandparenting time unless the grandparents can show that the denial poses a substantial risk of harm to the child.

QUICK LEGAL SUMMARY OF GRANDPARENTING TIME

Grandparents can only seek grandparenting time when:
- the parents are either divorced or were never married,

- the grandparent's child is deceased, or

- the child has not been placed for adoption.

Two fit parents can deny grandparenting time and prevent the grandparenting time motion from going forward.

Once the grandparents have demonstrated that they have standing to request grandparenting time, they must then prove by a preponderance of the evidence that the parent's denial of grandparenting time "creates a substantial risk of harm to the child's mental, physical, or emotional health." There is a presumption that a fit parent's decision to deny grandparenting time does not do so. The grandparent must rebut this presumption with evidence that the child will be harmed by denying grandparenting time. Once the grandparent rebuts the presumption, the trial judge must consider the best interests of the child.

The best-interest factors in the grandparenting time statute focus on the relationship between the child and grandparent:

a. The love, affection, and other emotional ties existing between the grandparent and the child.

b. The length and quality of the prior relationship between the child and the grandparent, the role performed by the grandparent, and the existing emotional ties of the child to the grandparent.

c. The grandparent's moral fitness.

d. The grandparent's mental and physical health.

e. The child's reasonable preference, if the court considers the child to be of sufficient age to express a preference.

f. The effect on the child of hostility between the grandparent and the parent of the child.

g. The willingness of the grandparent, except in the case of abuse or neglect, to encourage a close relationship between the child and the parent or parents of the child.

h. Any history of physical, emotional, or sexual abuse or neglect of any child by the grandparent.

i. Whether the parent's decision to deny, or lack of an offer of, grandparenting time is related to the child's well-being or is for some other unrelated reason.

j. Any other factor relevant to the physical and psychological well-being of the child.

PROBLEM AREAS IN GRANDPARENTING TIME DECISIONS

There are a remarkable number of published opinions in grandparenting time cases. Yet many issues remain unresolved.

THE HEAVY BURDEN OF PROVING SUBSTANTIAL RISK OF HARM.

Establishing a substantial risk of harm is difficult. In *Geering v Geering*, the Court of Appeals reversed the trial judge's decision awarding grandparenting time because the facts did not support a showing of substantial risk of harm. Although divorced, the parents agreed to deny grandparenting time. When two fit parents jointly oppose grandparenting time, this "effectively creates an irrebuttable presumption that denial of grandparenting time will *not* create a substantial risk of harm to the child." But the judge held a lengthy trial anyway to determine the parents' fitness. The trial judge decided they were not fit and ordered grandparenting time. The divorced parents, once again, joined forces to appeal.

The Court of Appeals reversed the trial judge's decision, stating that although the parents were not "perfect," the record "does not support a conclusion that either parent failed to adequately care for his or her children." Although the parents initially had trouble communicating with each other after the divorce, their coparenting skills had improved, the children were doing well emotionally and scholastically, and the children "witness[ed] their parents being respectful and pleasant for each other." Therefore, there was no basis to consider a request for grandparenting time.

EXPERT WITNESS TO PROVE
SUBSTANTIAL RISK OF HARM

There is a tremendous need for expert testimony to establish how the denial of grandparenting time harms the child. The statute does not explicitly require it, but judges find expert testimony helpful in deciding if grandparents have met their heavy burden, showing that the child will suffer a substantial risk of harm if denied contact with the grandparents.

> *There is a tremendous need for expert testimony to establish how the denial of grandparenting time harms the child.*

In *Keenan v Dawson*, the father was suspected of murdering the child's mother. After her death, he cut ties with the maternal grandparents. At the trial on grandparenting time, the grandparents presented an expert witness who opined that a substantial risk of harm would result from terminating grandparent visitation with the grandchild where the grandchild's mother had recently passed away. Both the grandparents' and the father's expert witnesses agreed that a child less than two years old would have very few concrete memories of his mother, but the grandparents' expert witness stated that by allowing grandparent visitation, the mother's memory would be "alive." The Court of Appeals said it is not enough for an expert witness to state that "grandparenting time is good." However, the grandmother's expert witness provided specific examples of what harm could ensue to the child by ending grandparent visitation. The Court of Appeals affirmed the trial judge's decision to award grandparenting time.

In *Hollis v Miller*, the maternal grandmother had maintained a close and continuous relationship with the child since birth. When the child was 2½ years old, the father began denying visitation with the mother's family. At trial, the only person to testify about the impact on the child of not having contact with the grandmother was the grandmother herself. There was no expert witness. Other witnesses testified about the close bond between the grandmother and the child. The trial judge awarded grandparenting time, and the father appealed. The Court of Appeals reversed the trial judge's decision because the grandmother had not produced sufficient evidence that the denial of grandparenting time would cause a substantial risk to the child. Her testimony was not enough. In addition, the Court of Appeals criticized the trial judge for not giving deference to the father's decision to deny grandparenting time. Even though the grandmother argued that the "child needs a loving grandparent and some access to the maternal side of the family," there was a missing piece to the puzzle. Unlike *Keenan*, there was no expert witness testimony stating the specific substantial harm the child may suffer if denied grandparent visitation.

Mackey v Benavides provides an example of how an expert witness's assistance can positively impact the case. In *Mackey*, the child and mother were living with the maternal grandparents for several years.

The father served in the US Navy and worked on a submarine off the coast of California. When the mother died unexpectedly, the father had his parents pick the child up right away, move her to their house, and enroll her in a new school. The paternal grandparents would not allow the maternal grandparents to see the child, ostensibly on the father's say-so. The maternal grandparents filed a motion for grandparenting time. An expert witness testified that a substantial risk of harm would come to "very young children who are abruptly removed from nonabusive caregivers with whom they are bonded" in conjunction with the death of a parent. Similar to *Keenan*, the expert witness in *Mackey* gave specific details about how a substantial risk of harm would result following the death of a parent. However, the expert witness had not been able to examine or meet with the grandchild. The expert's opinion was based on her professional experience and the testimony from the grandchild's kindergarten teacher and church pastor. The Court of Appeals concluded that the trial judge's findings that visitation was in the best interest of the child was not against the great weight of evidence standard and that the grandparents had overcome the presumption.

Appellate courts review the admission or denial of expert testimony for an abuse of discretion. That means it is very unlikely that the appellate courts will overturn a trial judge's decision to allow or exclude an expert's testimony.

> **PRACTICE TIP:** *When representing grandparents, you may need to file a motion for psychological evaluation of the child to allow your expert witness to evaluate the specific risk of harm if that child were not permitted visitation with your clients.*

THE VARIABILITY OF AN APPEAL BY RIGHT OF A GRANDPARENTING-TIME ORDER

There are two ways a grandparent can seek grandparenting time: by filing a new action or by filing a motion in an existing custody case. That very first decision has ramifications for both the parents' and grandparents' appeal rights. If the grandparents filed the request as a new action, then either the parent or grandparents may appeal the decision by right. But if the grandparents file a motion in an existing case, then neither they nor the parents will have an appeal by right under the 2019 final order court rule; instead, they must file an application for leave. (See chapter 1.) Grandparenting-time orders are now *excluded* from the class of postjudgment orders that are appealable by right.

There are other compelling reasons for *a parent* to have an appeal by right in the event the trial judge *grants* grandparenting time. In *Varran v Granneman*, discussing the former court rule, the Court of Appeals held:

> It cannot be disputed that a grandparenting-time order interferes with a parent's fundamental right to make decisions concerning the care, custody, and control of a child.... Because a grandparenting-time order overrides a parent's legal decision to deny grandparenting time, a grandparenting-time order interferes with a parent's fundamental right to make decisions concerning the care, custody, and control of his or her child.

Changing this court rule to include orders granting grandparenting time would help protect a parent's constitutional rights. In the meantime, parents can challenge the court rule on constitutional grounds when forced to file an application for leave to appeal.

GRANTING GRANDPARENTING TIME WITHOUT THE PROPER ANALYSIS OR FACT-FINDINGS

In *Falconer v Stamps*, the grandmother initially had guardianship over her grandchild while the parents were in Arizona. When they returned to Michigan, they sought to end the guardianship. Due to drug issues, the court created a plan for the mother, including drug screening and supervised visits. Just before the guardianship was set to end, the mother, the father, and the grandmother each filed motions for custody. Meanwhile, CPS was investigating issues in the grandmother's home. The trial judge awarded custody to the mother but allowed grandparenting time equivalent to parenting time for a noncustodial parent. The Court of Appeals overturned the trial judge's decision, awarding grandparenting time to a grandparent seeking third-party custody (discussed in chapter 8) when the grandparent didn't request it. The trial judge's decision "deprived [the parent] of the opportunity to argue that [the grandparents] had failed to rebut the presumption that [the parent's] decision did not create a substantial risk of harm."

Some courts seem to grant grandparenting time without any analysis whatsoever. In *Slocum v Floyd* (see "Amber's Story" in chapter 8), the parents had joint legal custody. The children lived primarily with their father and had parenting time with their mother. After the father died in a motorcycle crash, the grandparents filed a guardianship petition and then a third-party custody case. Although the trial judge correctly ruled that the mother retained sole legal custody of the children, the judge decided to grant the grandparents visitation—they had not requested it—without any evidence of a substantial risk of harm to the children, findings on the best interest of the children, or any of the other requirements under the grandparenting time statute. The Court of Appeals reversed the trial judge's grandparenting-time decision. The Court stated: "We thus conclude that the circuit court in this case erred when it awarded [the grandparents] grandparenting time after determining that [the mother] should receive full custody, without [the grandparents] having first moved for grandparenting time under MCL 722.27(b) and meeting the requirements of that statute." The Court criticized the trial judge for "conflat[ing] what should have been two separate and distinct actions"—a third-party custody case and grandparenting-time case.

UNRESOLVED ISSUES IN GRANDPARENTING TIME CASES

"PREPONDERANCE OF THE EVIDENCE" VERSUS "CLEAR AND CONVINCING EVIDENCE"

Some attorneys have argued that the grandparenting-time statute violates a parent's constitutional rights because it only requires a preponderance of the evidence. In *Varran v Granneman*, the father had been living with his parents until they asked him to leave due to their strained relationship. The grandchild continued to live with the grandparents full time for two more years, then for the next five years he spent weekends with his dad. After living with his grandparents for ten years, the child began to live with the father during the week but saw his grandparents every weekend. Eventually, the father restricted the grandparents' visitation with their grandchild, prompting them to file a motion for grandparenting time. The trial judge granted the motion, and the father appealed.

The Court of Appeals in *Varran* rejected the father's constitutional challenge to the statute's preponderance of evidence standard. The Court of Appeals held that the higher burdens included in the grandparenting-time statute were sufficient to protect a parent's rights. The Court stated:

> [B]ecause the grandparenting-time statute presumes that a fit parent's decision to deny grandparenting time does not create a substantial risk of harm to the child, and because it requires a grandparent to prove by a preponderance of the evidence that the parent's decision creates a substantial risk of harm to the child, the statute gives deference to the decisions of a fit parent. It does not allow the trial court to grant grandparenting time simply because it disagrees with the parent's decision.

The Court also said an award of grandparenting time is not much of an infringement on the parent's constitutional rights.

> Moreover, a parent's fundamental right to make decisions concerning the care, custody, and control of their children is not most at jeopardy when a grandparent petitions a court for grandparenting time. An order granting grandparenting time does not sever, permanently and irrevocably, a parent's parental rights to a child, and it remains subject to modification and termination. Therefore, we conclude that, because due process concerns are not at their highest in cases involving requests for grandparenting time, the requirement that grandparents, in order to rebut the presumption given to a fit parent's decision, prove by a preponderance of the evidence that the parent's decision to deny grandparenting time creates a substantial risk of harm to the child is sufficient to protect the fundamental rights of parents.

This analysis is very curious, because earlier *in the same opinion*, the Court of Appeals outlined why the grant of grandparenting time *does interfere* with the parent's constitutional right to direct the care, custody, and control of their children. The *Varran* Court seems to be saying that parents do have a fundamental liberty interest, but it is not such a high interest that it justifies the clear and convincing standard in grandparenting-time cases. These two conflicting holdings are difficult to reconcile. The Michigan Supreme Court has never addressed these important issues pertaining to the grandparenting time statute.

CAN A GRANDPARENT SEEK GRANDPARENTING TIME AFTER THEIR OWN CHILD'S RIGHTS TO THE GRANDCHILD WERE TERMINATED?

There seems to be much confusion over whether a grandparent whose own child's parental rights have been terminated still has standing to seek grandparenting time. In *Foster v Foster*, the Court of Appeals held that "[o]nce the rights of [the child's] biological parents were terminated by the family division, [the grandparent's] rights derivative of the parental relationship were also severed." However, in *Porter v Hill,* the Supreme Court issued an order (not an opinion) overturning the Court of Appeals for wrongly holding that "parents of a man whose parental right to his minor children were involuntarily terminated before his death did not have standing to seek grandparenting time with the children under the Child Custody Act," because "a biological parent is encompassed by the term 'natural parent' in MCL 722.22(e) and (h), regardless of whether the biological parent's parental rights have been terminated." Before that order, the traditional belief was that termination of a parent's rights cut off all familial ties; now it seems that does not occur until after a subsequent adoption.

INTERIM GRANDPARENTING-TIME ORDERS

The trial judge should not be able to enter an interim order in a grandparenting-time case before the grandparent has met the exacting standard of proving a substantial risk of harm to the child. But this is exactly what the trial judge did in *Repholz v Foster*. The child's parents were married when the father died. At first, the mother allowed the child to spend time with the paternal grandparents, but she stopped when the child became confused and stressed because the grandparents spent their time talking about his deceased father. The grandparents filed a motion for grandparenting time. The trial judge awarded grandparenting time solely based on the allegations in the petition and without hearing any evidence or making any findings required under the statute. The Court of Appeals reversed, but it would have been helpful for the *Foster* case to be published. Many of the issues raised in *Foster* and in *Mackey* have since been addressed in the published case of *Varran v Granneman*. However, the interim order issue has yet to be addressed in a published opinion.

TWO FIT PARENTS WHO OBJECT
TO GRANDPARENTING TIME

Two fit parents should not have to go through a fitness trial to deny grandparenting time. They are presumed to be fit when they come together and sign an affidavit asserting their parental rights. But that is exactly what happened in *Geering v Geering*. The divorced parents had to go through four days of evidentiary hearing, and the trial judge concluded that the parents were not fit and awarded grandparenting time over their objection. Rather than addressing the legal issue—that the parents were presumptively fit and their joint denial of grandparenting time should have denied the grandparents standing—

the Court of Appeals overturned the trial judge's decision on the merits (discussed above). It would have been helpful for the appellate courts to address the legal issue directly and hold that parents are presumed fit unless they have been adjudicated as unfit in a child welfare proceeding.

> **PRACTICE TIP:** *If you represent one or both parents who object to grandparenting time, consider filing a motion to dismiss for lack of standing in lieu of an answer. This will force the trial judge to address the legal issue of a joint denial first, before weighing the merits of the grandparents' case.*

HOW MUCH GRANDPARENTING TIME IS APPROPRIATE

The amount of grandparenting time a court can award is an open issue. Should a trial judge award more time to a grandparent time than it would give a noncustodial parent? That is what the trial judge did in *Keast*. The goal of grandparenting time is for the child to maintain a relationship with the grandparents, not to have the grandparents replace the parent. If the parent cannot care for their children, then there may be grounds for third-party custody (discussed in chapter 8) or guardianship (discussed in chapter 9). The Court of Appeals in *In re Keast* reversed the grandparenting-time decision on standing grounds, so the Court did not address the amount of grandparenting time awarded.

A PARENT'S DENIAL OF GRANDPARENTING TIME AS A PREREQUISITE OF THE GRANDPARENTS' MOTION

Does a parent actually need to deny grandparenting time before the grandparents can file their motion? What does it take for a parent to deny grandparenting time? The *Varran* Court did not require the grandparents to show their grandparenting time had been denied. This is curious because the statute refers to denial: "A fit parent's decision *to deny grandparenting time* does not create a substantial risk of harm to the child's mental, physical, or emotional health." It seems the *Varran* Court focused on the standing provision. Because a denial was not a preliminary requirement before filing a request for grandparenting time, and because the "deny" language only appeared in the section regarding rebutting the presumption, the Court found a grandparent could ask for grandparenting time even though the parent had not denied it. This remains an issue that should be addressed by the Michigan Supreme Court.

KEY TAKEAWAYS

- The goal of grandparenting time is for a child to maintain a relationship with his grandparents, not for the grandparents to take the place of the child's parents.

- A grandparent's case will be bolstered by an expert's testimony to help grandparents establish their burden.

- Establishing a substantial risk of harm to the child is no easy task, because parents need not be "perfect" to properly care for their children.

- Courts should not enter interim grandparenting orders without the evidence to support a substantial risk of harm to the child.

RESOURCES FOR CHAPTER SEVEN

GRANDPARENTING-TIME ERRORS

DeRose v DeRose, 469 Mich 320; 666 NW2d 636 (2003).

Foster v Foster, 237 Mich App 259; 602 NW2d 610 (1999).

Repholz v Foster, unpublished per curiam opinion of Court of Appeals, issued January 27, 2015 (Docket No. 322524).

Slocum v Floyd, unpublished per curiam opinion of Court of Appeals, issued June 19, 2018 (Docket Nos. 338782; 340242).

Varran v Granneman, 312 Mich App 591; 880 NW2d 242 (2015).

EXPERT TESTIMONY

Hollis v Miller, unpublished per curiam opinion of Court of Appeals, issued December 6, 2012 (Docket No. 306990).

Keenan v Dawson, 275 Mich App 671; 739 NW2d 681 (2007).

Mackey v Benavidez, unpublished per curiam opinion of Court of Appeals, issued September 9, 2014 (Docket No. 317146).

ADDITIONAL RESOURCES

Porter v Hill, unpublished per curiam opinion of Court of Appeals, issued June 11, 2013 (Docket No. 306562).

Speaker Law Firm, *7 Things You Should Know About Grandparenting Time Appeals* <https://bit.ly/2SrZVKL> (accessed June 11, 2021).

CHAPTER EIGHT

THIRD-PARTY CUSTODY

What It Takes to Raise Someone Else's Child

THE PURPOSE OF THIRD-PARTY CUSTODY

The courts presume that custody with a parent is in the best interests of the child. The fitness to parent your child is the "touchstone for invoking the constitutional protections of fundamental parental rights." When a parent is unfit, a third party must step in.

QUICK LEGAL SUMMARY OF THIRD-PARTY CUSTODY

For a nonparent to seek custody of a child, that nonparent must be the legal guardian or have a substantive right of entitlement to custody. Seeking third-party custody gives a guardian more decision-making authority since guardians are only allowed to make decisions regarding the child's health, safety, and welfare. However, the presumption in favor of maintaining the child's **established custodial environment** is outweighed by the parental presumption in the Child Custody Act—even when the child is not living with the parent. When a parent wants to regain custody, the nonparent should only retain custody where there is **clear and convincing evidence** that doing so is in the best interests of the child.

> **PRACTICE TIP:** *Consider whether third-party custody or guardianship is better for your client. A third-party custodian has more legal decision-making authority than a guardian, but it is easier to obtain guardianship.*

PROBLEM AREAS IN THIRD-PARTY CUSTODY DECISIONS

TENSION BETWEEN ESTABLISHED CUSTODIAL ENVIRONMENT AND PARENTAL PRESUMPTION

There are many examples where a child has been living with a nonparent for some time when the parent seeks to regain custody. In *Hunter v Hunter*, the parents had their children live with an aunt and uncle while they were dealing with a myriad of problems, including drug addiction and a prison sentence. Eventually, the parents started to turn their lives around. The aunt and uncle, who were already the children's guardians, filed a motion for custody. The mother objected, but the trial judge awarded third-party custody to the aunt

> *A third-party custodian has more legal decision-making authority than a guardian, but it is easier to obtain guardianship.*

and uncle. The case made its way to the Michigan Supreme Court, which reversed the trial judge's decision. The Supreme Court held that to protect a fit parent's fundamental constitutional rights, the presumption that children should be with their parents must trump the presumption against disrupting the children's established custodial environment with nonparents. In weighing these competing presumptions, the Supreme Court held that the third-party seeking custody must establish that it is not in the child's best interest for a parent to have custody by clear and convincing evidence.

Even when some of the best-interest factors favor the nonparent, that may not equate to clear and convincing evidence. In *Unthank v Wolfe,* the mother placed her child with a potential adopter when she felt she could not raise the child herself. After the child lived with the potential adoptive parents for many years, the case turned in a different direction, and they instead sought guardianship and then third-party custody. Then the child's mother sought to restore custody of the child. The trial judge weighed the best-interest factors and found in favor of the mother. Although many factors favored the intended adoptive parents, the parties were equal on several, and only one factor favored the mother: the nonparents still could not overcome their burden to keep the child with them, and the Court of Appeals affirmed the trial judge's decision.

STANDING TO SEEK THIRD-PARTY CUSTODY

What happens when a fit parent is not immediately available to care for a child? In *Kane v Anjoski,* the child lived with her father and stepmother. When the father passed away, the stepmother requested third-party custody. The mother had struggled with drugs and lived with an unstable boyfriend. Before his death, the father had gained sole physical custody, but the parents still shared joint legal custody.

The trial judge and Court of Appeals agreed that the stepmother did not have standing to seek custody. The stepmother was not the child's legal guardian, and the fact that the child had lived in the stepmother's home and perhaps even had an established custodial environment with the stepmother (and her father) did not grant her standing. The Court of Appeals noted that unless there had been legitimate allegations that the parent was unfit—such that the child was at risk of harm by going with the mother—the trial judge was required to return the child to the mother, the noncustodial parent.

> **PRACTICE TIP:** *Standing is often the main issue in a third-party custody case and must be supported by an affidavit filed with the complaint. Consider a motion for summary disposition in lieu of an answer if the third party has not properly established standing.*

PARENT DOES NOT NEED TO DEMONSTRATE PROPER CAUSE OR CHANGE IN CIRCUMSTANCES TO FILE A MOTION FOR CUSTODY

Unlike in disputes between two parents, when a child is with a third-party custodian, the parent can file a motion to regain custody without demonstrating proper cause or change in circumstances under *Vodvarka* (see chapter 3). In *Frowner v Smith*, the child lived with his grandparents after his mother died. Eventually, the father and grandparents agreed to a custody order sharing joint legal custody, setting the child's primary residence with the grandparents and awarding the father parenting time. Later, the father asked to change custody to him, alleging that the child would prefer to live with him and was not doing well in school. The trial judge rejected the father's motion because he had not established proper cause or change of circumstances under *Vodvarka*.

The Court of Appeals confronted the conflict between the parental presumption and the threshold requirements for custody modification. The Court found the balance tipped in favor of the parent:

> Conditioning an evidentiary hearing on a natural parent's ability to prove proper cause or changed circumstances effectively closes the courthouse doors whenever a child thrives in the care of a third party. Taken to its logical conclusion, as long as the status quo is generally maintained in the [third parties'] home, the circuit court's ruling precludes [the parent] from ever obtaining custody of his son.

The Court of Appeals reversed the trial judge's decision and remanded for an evidentiary hearing on the father's custody motion.

The difficulty with third-party custody cases under the Child Custody Act is that they are often decided with minimal recognition of the liberty interests at stake, and without the due process protections that are afforded when cases are brought pursuant to the probate or juvenile codes. From a parent's perspective, the only practical difference between a judge placing their child in the care of a third party in a child-protective proceeding versus a judge placing their child in the care of a third party under the Child Custody Act is that in the former situation, the parent gets an appointed lawyer and the child has the voice of a guardian ad litem, whereas in the latter the parent and child struggle alone. While Hunter and other cases have made it harder for a third party to convince our courts to destroy a child's parental relationship in custody cases, there is a long way to go before a parent's struggle isn't measured by the category of laws chosen for them by someone else.

—SARAPHOENA KOFFRON, attorney, Kalamazoo, MI

UNRESOLVED ISSUES IN THIRD-PARTY CUSTODY CASES

MISUSING A TEMPORARY GUARDIANSHIP ORDER TO FILE FOR THIRD-PARTY CUSTODY

Sometimes a person will wrongfully obtain a temporary guardianship order and then use that guardianship as standing grounds to file a third-party custody action. This occurred in *Floyd* (see "Amber's Story"), where the grandparents convinced the trial judge to grant them a temporary guardianship without a hearing, then used the temporary guardianship as a basis to file a third-party custody action before the probate judge could hear the mother's objection to the guardianship. Once the third-party custody action was filed, the probate court lost jurisdiction, making it extremely difficult for the mother to challenge the underlying guardianship in either court or on appeal.

This topic was also addressed in *Unthank* (discussed above), where the Court of Appeals held that the third-party custodian did not have standing to pursue custody because the guardianship had been improperly entered. But the Supreme Court in *Unthank* vacated that portion of the Court of Appeals's decision. The takeaway, then, from *Unthank* and *Floyd* is that even if a third party fraudulently obtains a temporary guardianship, that guardianship gives the nonparent standing to bring a third-party custody action. The parent cannot then challenge the underlying guardianship's defects in the third-party custody case. That is unsettling, but it is the current state of the law until an appellate court tells us otherwise.

AMBER'S STORY:
After Her Ex-Husband Died, His Parents Stole the Kids

After her divorce, Amber had some CPS issues, which she resolved. She enjoyed frequent parenting time with her children and had joint legal custody with her ex-husband. But when her ex-husband died unexpectedly, his parents came to the funeral and took the children away. Amber asked the police for help, but they would not get involved in a "family dispute." The grandparents obtained a temporary guardianship, even though they did not have standing (see chapter 9). Amber objected, but before the hearing date, the grandparents rushed to circuit court to file a third-party custody complaint, which stopped the guardianship case. For three months, Amber was unable to have any contact with her children until finally the circuit court recognized her as sole legal custodian, and the kids went home. In a curious move, the judge awarded grandparenting time—even though they did not request it—without any of the required findings (see chapter 7).

The whole ordeal made Amber feel "like [she] had no rights, that [she] was unimportant, and they were not interested in the family unit itself." There was a lot of anger and hurt, especially since the judge did not follow the law and made a decision without "considering my natural rights of raising one's child, which falls within the Constitution."

It was horrible for the kids, who had just lost their father, that Amber "wasn't able to be there for them, to console them, and they still have anger toward [her] for not being there." Amber said, "I feel like everything that happened, that I had no control over, caused irreparable harm to my kids, both emotionally and mentally." Once she regained custody, the judge acted like Amber "should be satisfied with that, and I should be OK with grandparenting time that was errone-ously granted with no basis."

KEY TAKEAWAYS

- A parent can file a motion to change custody from the third party to the parent *without* a showing of proper cause or change in circumstances, under the *Vodvarka* standard.

- A third party seeking custody must establish by clear and convincing evidence that it is not in the child's best interest for a parent to have custody. Even where some of the best-interest factors favor the third party, that may not meet that evidentiary burden if the third party and parent are equal on several factors.

RESOURCES FOR CHAPTER EIGHT

THIRD-PARTY STANDING

Bowie v Arder, 190 Mich App 571; 476 NW2d 649 (1991).

In re Anjoski, 283 Mich App 41; 770 NW2d 1 (2009).

Terry v Aflum, 237 Mich App 522; 603 NW2d 788 (1999).

Unthank v Wolfe, 282 Mich App 40; 763 NW2d 287 (2008).

Unthank v Wolfe, 483 Mich 964, 763 NW2d 924 (2009).

MCL 722.26(b).

MCL 722.26(c).

PROVING THIRD-PARTY CUSTODY

Eldred v Ziny, 246 Mich App 142; 631 NW2d 748 (2001).

Frowner v Smith, 296 Mich App 374; 820 NW2d 235 (2012).
MCL 722.25.

CHAPTER NINE

GUARDIANSHIPS

Providing a Child a Safe Place
When a Parent Needs Help

THE PURPOSE OF GUARDIANSHIPS

Guardianships are designed to keep children in a safe home when parents are unable to care for them and to give caretakers legal authority over the children in the parent's absence.

QUICK LEGAL SUMMARY OF GUARDIANSHIP

There are different types of guardianships, depending on whether the parent left the child with someone without legal authority or is seeking a guardian for their child.

EPIC guardianships are created under the Estate and Protected Individuals Code. They can be temporary or full guardianships. Typically, an EPIC guardianship is used when a parent leaves the child with a caretaker without giving them legal authority over the child's care and maintenance. An EPIC guardianship gives the parent fewer rights and does not require a parenting plan. Either party can ask to modify these guardianships based on the best interests of the children. Even if a trial judge denies the parent's request to modify or terminate the guardianship, the parent can bring the motion again later.

A Limited Guardianship is formed by agreement between the parent and caretaker. It includes a parenting plan that allows the parent to maintain a relationship with their child. However, if the parent does not comply with the requirements of the limited guardianship, the guardian can seek termination of the parent's rights.

A Juvenile Guardianship is a relatively new feature of the Juvenile Code. It allows the court in an abuse and neglect case to place a child with a guardian instead of terminating parental rights (see chapter 12). Trial judges typically use juvenile guardianships if they determine that the child should not return home, but termination is not appropriate. Juvenile guardianship should only be used when the child and parent cannot be reunified, or when adoption is not a viable option. The parent cannot seek to terminate a juvenile guardianship; that can only be done by the trial judge, Department of Health and Human Services (DHHS), or the **L-GAL**.

NICK'S STORY:

Children Are Split Up Once Mother Dies, Even after Father Is Released from Prison

Nick made mistakes and served time in a Texas prison. While he was there, the mother of his children passed away, and he placed the children with his mother. Nick's mom is a nurse, and she worked very hard to keep the girls safe and secure. But the trial judge granted a coguardianship between the paternal grandmother, maternal grandfather, and maternal stepgrandmother, granting these people, living in three different households, joint legal custody. When Nick was released from prison, he wanted to return home to be with his children, but the judge refused to end the guardianship. Rather than keeping the girls with their grandparents, the judge allowed the older daughter to live with an aunt, while the younger daughter lived with her stepgrandmother.

While Nick and his younger daughter remain very close, Nick is worried that the older child will have emotional problems as she gets older; she is torn between her families and feels like she has to pick sides—to the point where she does not even feel like she can give her dad a hug in front of her mother's family.

Nick felt the judge was unfair and unwilling to give Nick a chance to parent his children, since Nick had appeared before him as a juvenile. Even though several more years have gone by, Nick does not feel as though he will get a fair hearing with this judge.

PROBLEM AREAS IN GUARDIANSHIP DECISIONS

DID THE PARENT GRANT PERMISSION FOR THE CHILDREN TO STAY WITH THE CARETAKER?

In *Deschaine v St. Germain*, the mother was living with her parents and her child. When the mother passed away, the father came to the funeral and tried to pick up the kids, but the grandfather would not let him. The grandfather then filed for guardianship, which the trial judge granted. The Court of Appeals overturned the trial judge's decision because the father never gave permission for the children to stay with the grandparents.

WHEN A GUARDIAN WANTS TO SEEK TERMINATION OF PARENTAL RIGHTS SO THAT THE GUARDIAN CAN ADOPT THE CHILD

In *In re Long*, a grandmother became the guardian of her grandchildren after their mother died. The grandmother wanted to terminate the putative father's parental rights under the Juvenile Code so that she could adopt her grandchildren. The Court of Appeals concluded that the man had to be a legal father before she could seek to terminate his rights. This case creates problems for guardians because if the putative father is unknown, his rights can never be terminated under the Juvenile Code. Once a known putative father becomes the legal father, the Juvenile Code still requires the guardian to prove that he failed to support or contact the child for two years before his parental rights can be terminated. The only remaining alternative would be to ask DHHS to pursue termination of the legal father's parental rights for abandoning his child. (See chapter 12, "Termination of Parental Rights.")

*It is concerning and unfair when the courts try to fashion
a remedy even though the law is not there to support it.
The whole purpose of the law is supposed to point toward
reunification unless it's not in the child's best interest. We
need to at least give the parent a shot at reunification.*

—KRISTEN WOLFRAM, attorney, Grand Rapids, MI

WHICH BEST-INTEREST FACTORS TO USE IN GUARDIANSHIP CASES

Neither the Juvenile Code nor EPIC provides statutory best-interest factors for the creation, modification, or termination of guardianship. Courts have looked to the Child Custody Act for guidance (see chapter 2). In *In re COH*, the Supreme Court used the Child Custody Act because the relevant Juvenile Code provision did not apply any particular set of factors to determine the best interests of the child. The Court suggested that the Adoption Code's best-interest factors might be appropriate too. In *Hunter v Hunter*, the guardianship was created under EPIC, but the judge also used the Child Custody Act to determine the child's best interests.

UNRESOLVED ISSUES IN GUARDIANSHIP CASES

IS TEMPORARY PLACEMENT ENOUGH?

In *In re Orta*, a young mother had two children and left them with their grandmother for certain periods of time, giving her the children's clothing and supplies, a signed statement consenting to emergency or general medical treatment, their health insurance cards, and her telephone number. Eventually the mother tried to pick her children up, but the grandmother did not want to return them. Four months after the mother dropped off her children, the grandmother filed a petition for guardianship, which the trial judge granted. The mother got her life together and eventually had the ability to care for her children. She tried to terminate the guardianship twice: in 2016 and 2018. Both times the trial judge refused. She appealed the second denial.

The Court of Appeals concluded that the grandmother never had a basis for guardianship because the mother never meant for the children to live permanently with the grandmother. The Court of Appeals relied on *Deschaine* (discussed above), which said that guardianship is appropriate if a parent permits the child to "permanently reside with someone else." The *Orta* Court emphasized the temporary nature of the original agreement: the mother originally asked for help for about one month's time. After the month had passed, the parties agreed that the grandmother would continue to care for the children until the mother moved into her apartment. "Again, this was a temporary arrangement, and [the mother] leased her apartment effective October 1, 2015." In the Court of Appeals's view, once the mother moved into that apartment, the children should have returned to her, eliminating the need for guardianship. The Court of Appeals did not explain what the "temporary" standard is or how long a "temporary" placement can last. The Supreme Court has heard oral argument on the grandmother's application for leave to appeal and is examining "whether to establish guardianship, a parent must intend that her child permanently resides with another person." The mother's plight in *Orta* evokes sympathy, but it is not clear how a caretaker would be able to prove that the arrangement was intended to be "permanent."

> **PRACTICE TIP:** *Be sure to include evidence of the permanency of placement in support of your petition for guardianship, such as where the children were enrolled in school, where their medical providers were located, or how the parent told the children to refer to the potential guardian.*

DOES THE FACT THAT THE CHILDREN ARE IN A GUARDIANSHIP PLACEMENT MEAN THAT THE PARENT IS UNFIT?

In *In re Versalle*, the father had two children. The children and their mother lived with the paternal grandmother. The mother passed away, and the children continued to live with the grandmother due to the father's insecure housing situation. The father completed mental health treatment, got back on his feet, and moved to Texas. The children visited him there during school breaks and for an entire summer. But when the father told his mother that he wanted the kids to live with him, the grandmother filed for guardianship the day before the scheduled pickup. The trial judge granted guardianship. The Court of Appeals held that the "parental presumption" of the Child Custody Act applied to guardianship cases—that is, there is a presumption that is in the best interest of the child to live with a parent. The Court said, "A parent does not lose his or her constitutional right that would be afforded in a child custody case just because the parent is part of a guardianship proceeding instead of a custody case." Yet the Court of Appeals upheld the trial judge's decision and concluded that the father was not fit because he granted permission for the children to stay with the grandmother without giving her legal authority to care for them. The Supreme Court has ordered oral argument in *Versalle* and is examining whether EPIC's guardianship provision is constitutional because "it does not allow for a presumption that a fit parent's decision is in the best interests of the child."

GRANTING A CARETAKER "LEGAL AUTHORITY" OVER THE CHILD

It is not currently clear what it takes for a parent to grant a caretaker "legal authority" in a way that will prevent that caretaker from obtaining guardianship. In *Trudeau v Martin*, the parent gave the caretaker power of attorney. This is a simple form, often prepared without an attorney's assistance. The caretaker filed for guardianship, and the trial judge denied the request, finding that the power of attorney denied him jurisdiction. The caretaker appealed. The Court of Appeals ruled in his favor and reversed the trial judge. It held that the power of attorney did not divest the trial judge of jurisdiction, because such forms are only effective for six months. When the power of attorney expired, the caretaker's legal authority to care for the children terminated, leaving him without any "legal power, authority, or obligation with regard to the welfare of the child." The power of attorney "did not address the long-term needs of the children and, therefore, a guardianship proceeding was appropriate to ensure their well-being."

KEY TAKEAWAYS

- Guardianships are meant to keep children in safe homes if the parents are unable to care for their children and allow the caretaker to have legal authority over the children.

- EPIC guardianships are typically used when a parent leaves the child with a caretaker *without* providing that caretaker with legal authority over the child.

- Limited guardianships require a <u>parenting plan</u> that ensures that the parent will be able to maintain a relationship with the child.

- Current case law is unclear as to what it takes for a parent to <u>grant legal authority</u> to a caretaker in a way that will prevent that caretaker from obtaining guardianship.

- An appellate court should overturn guardianship when the parent *did not grant permission* for their children to stay with that caretaker.

RESOURCES FOR CHAPTER NINE

EPIC GUARDIANSHIP

Hunter v Hunter, 484 Mich 247; 771 NW2d 694 (2009).
MCL 700.5204.

POWER OF ATTORNEY

Trudeau v Martin, 237 Mich App 253; 602 NW2d 630 (1999).
MCL 700.405.

JUVENILE CODE GUARDIANSHIPS

In re COH, 495 Mich 184; 848 NW2d 107 (2014).

In re Long, 326 Mich App 455; 927 NW2d 724 (2018).

MCL 700.5205.

MCL 712A.19(a).

MCL 712A.19(c).

GUARDIANSHIP IMPACTS

Deschaine v St. Germain, 256 Mich App 665; 671 NW2d 79 (2003).

In re Orta, unpublished per curiam opinion of Court of Appeals, issued February 4, 2020 (Docket Nos. 346399; 346400).

In re Versalle, unpublished per curiam opinion of Court of Appeals, issued October 15, 2020 (Docket Nos. 351757 and 351758).

CHAPTER TEN

ADOPTION

The Fight to Create a New Family

THE PURPOSE OF THE ADOPTION CODE

THE ADOPTION CODE IDENTIFIES FIVE CORE PURPOSES FOCUSED ON THE CHILD'S PERMANENCY, STABILITY, AND BEST INTERESTS:

a. To ensure adoptees receive the services they need.

b. To safeguard and promote adoptees' rights and best interests as paramount while also protecting the rights of all parties concerned.

c. To place the adoptees with adoptive families as quickly as possible.

d. To achieve permanency and stability for adoptees as quickly as possible.

e. To allow all interested parties to participate in adoption proceedings so that, once finalized, each adoption will be permanent.

QUICK LEGAL SUMMARY OF ADOPTION LAW

There are three main types of contested adoption cases. Each type has its own set of statutory requirements, its own problem areas, and its own unresolved issues.

Section 39 cases arise when an unmarried mother arranges for direct placement, selecting a family to adopt her newborn baby. Often these children are the result of short-term relationships (such as one-night stands) between their parents. Before the adoption can be finalized, the trial judge must terminate the rights of any putative father—that is, any man the biological mother believes could be the father. However, Section 39 only applies to do-nothing fathers. If that man is a "do-something" father, one who provided substantial and regular support to the mother and child or has an established a custodial relationship with the child, then his rights can only be terminated without his consent under the Juvenile Code (for abuse and neglect) or in a stepparent adoption. Section 39 only looks at the father's actions during the pregnancy and the ninety days before he received the notice of the adoption hearing. Direct placement adoption petitions are typically filed shortly after the baby's birth, so the putative father generally needs to "do something" during the pregnancy to demonstrate his commitment to raising his child. If, on the other hand, the man is a do-nothing father, then he must appear in court, object to the adoption, and request custody of the child. He must prove that he is fit and able to parent the child, and that custody with him is in the child's best interests. If not, then his parental rights can be terminated to make way for the adoption.

Section 45 hearings typically occur when the parent's rights have already been terminated (usually for abuse and neglect under the Juvenile Code) and a prospective adoptive family is denied consent to adopt. The Michigan Children's Institute (MCI)—the ward for all foster children in the state of Michigan—reviews adoption requests and decides who should adopt the child. If MCI denies consent to a prospective adopter, then they can file a motion under Section 45 of the Adoption Code to have a judge review that decision. The prospective adopter must demonstrate that MCI's decision to deny consent was arbitrary and capricious by clear and convincing evidence.

Stepparent adoptions occur when one parent's spouse wants to become the legal parent of their stepchildren. First, the other parent's rights must be terminated under the Adoption Code by showing that for two or more years, the other parent has failed to provide substantial and regular support and has failed to have substantial and regular contact with the child. To pursue a stepparent adoption, the petitioning parent must have custody by way of a court order. That means that if the father is considered the "legal father" due to an acknowledgment of parentage, the mother will not be able to ask for a stepparent adoption, nor will she be able to use the stepparent adoption to terminate the rights of a putative father.

Family court judges are often unfamiliar with the Michigan Adoption Code and therefore interpret its provisions as suggestions rather than mandatory statutory requirements. The unfortunate result is frequent adjournments of critical hearings and inappropriate focus on the rights of persons other than the adoptee, whose interests in permanency and stability should be paramount and superior to those of all other parties. We find, at the trial level, that referees and judges simply do not appreciate the emotional and financial consequences of postponing adoptions to accommodate the schedules of hearing participants or their own busy dockets. Attorneys whose practices include adoptions understand that these proceedings take precedence over their other business and personal commitments.

—**DONNA MEDINA**, attorney, Birmingham, MI

PROBLEM AREAS IN ADOPTION DECISIONS

SECTION 39 PROBLEMS

ADJOURNING AN ADOPTION CASE IN
FAVOR OF A PATERNITY CASE

Filing a notice of intent to claim paternity, or even a paternity action, does not qualify a man as a do-something father under Section 39. However, some trial judges will allow the paternity case to proceed first if there is good cause to adjourn the adoption case. This allows the putative father to obtain an order of filiation, making him the legal father, and interfere with the adoption, even if he did not do anything to support the baby or mother before the adoption case began. The tension between the Adoption Code and the Paternity Act has come up in numerous cases, the most significant ones being *In re MKK* and *In re MGR*.

In *MKK*, the mother and father had a short-term relationship resulting in pregnancy. Once the father learned that the mother was pregnant, he tried to send money to her and then her attorney. He took parenting classes and prepared his home for a newborn, purchasing a crib, high chair, and car seats. Once the baby was born, the mother placed the child with a prospective adoptive family. The putative father filed a paternity case and asked the adoption judge (in a different court) to adjourn the adoption case so he could obtain DNA testing. At the same time, the mother asked the paternity judge to stay the paternity case while the adoption was pending. The paternity case was adjourned, but the adoption case was not. Ultimately, after the Section 39 hearing, the trial judge decided it was not in the child's best interests for the father to have custody but still denied the adoption petition. Everyone appealed.

The Court of Appeals created a three-part test for showing good cause to adjourn when there are competing paternity and adoptions cases:

- There is no doubt that the putative father is the biological father of the child;

- the putative father filed a paternity action without unreasonable delay; and

- There is no direct evidence that the putative father filed the paternity action simply to thwart the adoption proceedings.

Although this test from *MKK* has been challenged several times, the Supreme Court called it an "admirable effort by the Court of Appeals to balance the competing rights, interest, and responsibilities of the parties" when there are competing adoption and paternity cases.

PRACTICE TIP: *There are at least seven things that many trial judges consistently do wrong in adoption cases:*

1. *Ordering a DNA test or asking a putative father if he wants to "contest the adoption" (the Adoption Code does not allow the court to order a DNA test).*

2. *Failing to require putative fathers to unequivocally ask for custody of the child to avoid termination of his rights.*

3. *Failing to prioritize the child's rights over conflicting rights of another party, particularly a putative father.*

4. *Appointing an attorney before the putative father asks for one and without determining whether he can retain counsel or plans to object to the adoption.*

5. *Granting adjournments rather than terminating the putative father's rights (as required by the Adoption Code) if he doesn't show up at a hearing.*

6. *Giving do-nothing putative fathers the same rights and protections as do-something putative fathers and legal fathers.*

7. *Failing to penalize discovery violations or enforce court orders, thus delaying the proceedings and interfering with the adoptee's stability and permanency.*

In *In re MGR* (discussed more below), the trial judge for both the adoption and paternity cases, on her own initiative, adjourned the adoption case so the putative father could obtain DNA testing and establish his paternity. The judge did so without applying the *MKK* analysis. After the prospective adopters appealed the adjournment, the trial judge issued a supplemental order going through the *MKK* factors. Eventually, the Supreme Court reversed the decision to adjourn the adoption case and criticized the trial judge for failing to adjourn the paternity case. Had the trial judge properly moved forward with the adoption case, she would have evaluated the child's best interests much sooner under the Adoption Code. Instead, she allowed the putative father to obtain a paternity order, dragging the case out, and only considered the child's best interests after the case was remanded by the Supreme Court.

MICHAEL'S STORY:
Persevering to Create a Family despite Numerous Obstacles

Michael and his wife wanted a family and worked with an unwed pregnant mother for an adoption. The baby came home with them from the hospital. The biological father had done nothing to support the mother during her pregnancy, but he objected to the adoption because he did not want "strangers" raising his child. He did not want to raise the child himself either. Instead he wanted either the mother or one of his aunts to raise the child. The adoption trial took eighteen months! The judge highlighted many negative facts about the putative father but still found a way to deny the adoption. The judge said that although the putative father had not shown any level of commitment in his whole life, the judge believed he would muddle through adequately for this child.

At the same time, the judge in the paternity case did not understand adoption law. The Court of Appeals had allowed Michael and his wife to keep the child in their home while they appealed the Section 39 order, but the paternity case judge ordered Michael to hand the eighteen-month-old child over to the biological parents the baby had never met, even while ordering that both parents' time with the child must be supervised by their own family members at all times. It took a week of emergency appellate filings before the child came back home to Michael and his wife.

"It was incredibly difficult to watch him grow, have us fall more in love, and not just the idea of having a child but genuinely having the connection with this child and witnessing the milestones at three months, six months, nine months, eighteen months and beyond." Michael and his wife wrestled with two things: "(1) How do we compartmentalize these feelings to protect this child because he deserves to grow up in a stable environment without anxiety, and (2) how do we guard ourselves if the law gets this completely wrong and we don't win our appeal to adopt this child?" The Supreme Court reversed the adoption court, and the Court of Appeals reversed the paternity court. Now Michael's family is whole.

PRACTICE TIP: *Either the biological mother or the prospective adopters can appeal an adoption order granting an adjournment and, if a motion was filed in the paternity court, also appeal a paternity order denying a stay of the paternity case.*

SECTION 45 PROBLEMS

The main problem with cases under Section 45 is the near-impossible burden posed by the statute. A prospective adopter must prove MCI's decision to deny consent to adopt was arbitrary and capricious by clear and convincing evidence. This is perhaps the most onerous standard in Michigan. It is rare for a trial judge faced with a Section 45 hearing to reach that conclusion, because MCI only needs "any good reason" to deny consent. When it has happened, the appellate courts have frequently reversed to keep MCI's decision in place.

One exception was in *In re RC*. An aunt wanted to adopt her niece who had been living with her for several years. The aunt dropped the child off at the grandparents' home so she could run errands for an hour, and the child and another toddler escaped the house and were found outside by police. No one was harmed, but CPS removed the child from her aunt's care and placed her with a foster family. Both the aunt and the foster family sought to adopt the little girl. The MCI superintendent favored the foster family based on its belief that (1) the aunt lacked honesty and credibility; (2) CPS had substantiated claims of neglect against the aunt and placed her on the central registry; and (3) the aunt's foster care license had been revoked. The trial judge found that MCI's decision was arbitrary and capricious.

The foster parents appealed. According to the Court of Appeals, much of the information on which the MCI superintendent relied was "false and misleading," and the superintendent "should have been aware" the information was inaccurate. In particular, the Court of Appeals pointed out the MCI superintendent sent an email to the Foster Care Review Board, in which she stated that she "will be denying [the petitioner's] consent to adopt [RC]." MCI made this "unequivocal statement" before conducting a full investigation and before the aunt had an "opportunity to respond to all the faulty claims that had been made regarding her." Based on MCI's emailed statement, the Foster Care Review Board denied the aunt's appeal of its removal decision. The Court of Appeals held that the trial judge "did not clearly err by finding that the superintendent's reasons for denying consent to adopt were arbitrary and capricious."

> **PRACTICE TIP:** *Prospective adopters should hire an attorney early and not wait until MCI denies consent to adopt. Before MCI makes its decision, the attorney should be prepared to proactively demonstrate to MCI that other information from an agency or caseworker is false or misleading.*

STEPPARENT ADOPTION PROBLEMS

The Legislature needs to revise the stepparent adoption provisions of the Adoption Code to correct unintended consequences of a recent amendment. Previously, this statute gave "*the* parent with legal custody" standing to petition the court for stepparent adoption. The Supreme Court in *In re AJR* decided that use of the phrase "*the* parent with legal custody" meant that a petitioner parent must have *sole* legal custody. Because so many trial judges around this state award joint legal custody, even to uninvolved parents, the *AJR* decision impacted many parents' ability to seek stepparent adoptions even when the other parent had not provided any support or not had any contact with the child for more than two years.

After *AJR,* the Legislature amended the statute and inadvertently made other changes that caused new problems. The statute now gives standing to "a parent having custody of the child according to a court order." In *In re AGD*, there was no custody order. The child's legal father had signed an affidavit of parentage, making him the legal father, but he had been completely uninvolved for three years. The Court of Appeals said the mother did not have standing to file the stepparent adoption petition because her custody was not "according to a court order." This decision impacts every parent who never needed a custody order before; that is, unwed mothers. It also prevents stepparent adoptions in cases with putative fathers, because there can be no custody order where there is no legal father. The drafters never intended to create this loophole in the revised statutory language.

> **PRACTICE TIP:** *To satisfy AGD's reading of the amended statute, when representing a mother with a putative father or an affidavit of parentage, you may want to ask the trial judge to explicitly reserve the issue of child support in light of the pending adoption. This will avoid creating a low child support order or triggering an automatic income withholding order that will interfere with the termination of the father's rights.*

UNRESOLVED ISSUES IN ADOPTION CASES

SECTION 39 UNRESOLVED ISSUES

GOOD CAUSE TO ADJOURN HIGHEST PRIORITY ADOPTION CASES

Trial judges should always remember that adoption cases have the highest priority on their dockets. They should not be delayed for any other types of cases, even a competing paternity action. According to the Adoption Code:

> All proceedings under this chapter shall be considered to have *the highest priority* and *shall be advanced on the court docket* so as to provide for their *earliest practicable disposition.*

Trial judges should always remember that adoption cases have the highest priority on their dockets.

The Adoption Code requires good cause to adjourn adoption proceedings. They should not be pushed out for months, as domestic cases often are. These types of delays interfere with the permanency and stability of the child, one of the Adoption Code's main purposes. What might good cause look like (beyond death or illness of an attorney or witness)? Even after *MGR* (sua sponte adjournment so the putative father could establish paternity) and *MKK* (with its amorphous three-part test), the answer is still unclear.

CAN A PATERNITY ORDER MAKE AN ADOPTION APPEAL MOOT?

When a trial judge denies an adoption, for example, by finding that the putative father is a do-something father under Section 39, or because it is in the child's best interests to have custody with the father, the mother or prospective adoptive parents can file an appeal. Sometimes the putative father obtains a paternity order while the adoption appeal is pending. The Court of Appeals has said that this paternity order makes the adoption appeal moot. However, the Supreme Court disagreed.

In *MGR*, the same judge presided over the adoption and paternity actions. She stayed the adoption case sua sponte and denied the biological mother's multiple requests to stay the paternity case so the adoption case could proceed first. In *LMB*, the two actions were presided over by different judges. The paternity judge refused to stay that action while the adoption case was pending on appeal. In both cases, the Court of Appeals held that the subsequent entry of a paternity order made each adoption appeal moot. The Supreme Court reversed both Court of Appeals's decisions because had a stay of the paternity actions been granted—as requested by the biological mother in *MGR* and the prospective adopters in *LMB*—then no order of filiation would have entered. For both cases, the Supreme Court did not remand to the Court of Appeals for a decision on the merits—which it normally would do. Instead it remanded both cases directly to the trial courts. In *MGR*, the remand was for the trial judge in the adoption case to conduct a best-interest hearing under Section 39. In *LMB*, the Supreme Court ordered the adoption judge to terminate the putative father's parental rights, finding the judge's determination that custody with the putative father was in the child's best interests to be an abuse of discretion based on the facts.

The Supreme Court noted that *MGR* and *LMB* do not create a per se rule that a paternity order can never render an adoption appeal moot. Both decisions relied heavily on the facts in each case. The Supreme Court suggested the Legislature should take action. Thus it is still unclear when the Court of Appeals may hold that an adoption appeal is moot.

PERSONAL ATTENDANCE AT A SECTION 39 HEARING

In *MGR*, the putative father did not show up for the Section 39 hearing. His attorney appeared on his behalf to object and request custody. The prospective adopters challenged the trial judge's decision to accept the attorney's appearance when the putative father did not bother to show up for court. The Court of Appeals said the attorney's appearance was good enough. This should be challenged in future cases, or the Legislature should fix the statute. Typically in a Section 39 case, the putative father must testify to demonstrate he is fit and able to take care of a child and that custody with him is in the child's best interests. If a man is not able or willing to personally attend a court hearing about the future of a child who he claims he wants to raise, how can the trial judge have any confidence that that man is fit and able to take care of the child for the next eighteen years?

CONDITIONAL REQUESTS FOR CUSTODY

A putative father is required to request custody to obtain a Section 39 hearing under the Adoption Code. If he does not, the trial judge can terminate his right immediately. But many times, a putative father will say that he wants custody of the child if he turns out to be the biological father. The Adoption Code does not say that the man can make a conditional request, nor does it include a mechanism for DNA testing. For that, the putative father must file a paternity action. To object to an adoption, a putative father must stand up and say that he is willing to be responsible for the child's health, safety, and welfare for the next eighteen years based on the fact that he engaged in sexual relations with the child's mother. If he is unwilling to do that, then he should not be permitted to interfere with the child's permanency.

SPORADIC OR LIMITED-DURATION SUPPORT

To be considered a do-something father, the putative father must show he provided substantial and regular support to the mother during her pregnancy. If he did, then the adoption cannot be finalized under Section 39. There are plenty of cases discussing what substantial support is (a place to live, a payment of several hundred dollars per month) and what it is not (a pack of diapers, a cell phone, twenty dollars for gas, a ride to a doctor appointment), but less guidance on whether that substantial support is "regular." Because the statute requires both substantial and regular support, the putative father should provide substantial support through most if not all of the pregnancy. There are many cases where the putative father provided substantial support for the first three months of the pregnancy—until the mother left him. One trimester of support is not regular. The Court of Appeals should clarify what it takes to have both substantial and regular support.

SECTION 45 UNRESOLVED ISSUES

TIMING AND THE ABILITY TO FILE A REQUEST FOR A SECTION 45 HEARING

There are many problems with Section 45 of the Adoption Code, but one unresolved issue is the notice prospective adopters receive that MCI has denied consent to their adoption and how that notice impacts their ability to challenge that denial in a Section 45 hearing. According to the Adoption Code, a Section 45 hearing cannot be requested more than fifty-six days after the child's placement with another family or after the adoption order is entered. But the statute does not give an actual time frame in which to file the Section 45 request. Many times, MCI mails its denial to the denied adopter shortly before an adoption with another family occurs. Denied adopters do not receive notice of competing adoption hearings, so even if they move quickly, a finalized adoption could prevent them from challenging MCI's decision.

In *In re OFF*, a grandmother who had been raising her grandchild for years was denied MCI consent. It did not take her long to file the Section 45 request, but by the time she did, the trial judge had already finalized the adoption with another family. The grandmother challenged the trial judge's decision and the fact that the statute denied her due process of law because it did not give her notice or an opportunity to be heard. (See chapter 1.) The Court of Appeals simply said that she could have filed her request sooner (in less than fourteen days)—even though she had no notice of the adoption hearing, and even though she had to find an attorney to gather evidence to demonstrate that MCI acted arbitrarily and capriciously. The Court of Appeals's comments ignore how difficult it is to find an adoption attorney willing to take on a Section 45 case, gather the evidence and law, and file the Section 45 petition.

STEPPARENT ADOPTION UNRESOLVED ISSUES

NEWLY ENTERED CUSTODY OR SUPPORT ORDERS

AGD's ruling means mothers seeking stepparent adoptions must first obtain child custody orders, which are ordinarily accompanied by child support orders. When analyzing a stepparent adoption request, the trial judge can ignore a judgment that reserves child support or sets that number to zero. However, that may not be an option if the mother is receiving public assistance. It is unknown how judges will treat these newly obtained child support orders in deciding whether the father failed to support the child.

HAVING THE ABILITY TO SUPPORT OR HAVE CONTACT WITH THE CHILD

The statute only requires a respondent parent to substantially support the child or substantially maintain contact with the child if doing so is within that parent's ability. So what does it mean to be able? Is an incarcerated parent forgiven for not supporting or contacting the child? Couldn't that incarcerated parent send small presents, cards, or a portion of their in-custody earnings? What about when the petitioner parent has a Personal Protection Order (PPO) against the other parent? Does that prevent the respondent parent from sending money through his attorney, a family member, or mutual friend? Often PPOs will prohibit written or electronic communications along with physical contact. Is a parent able to maintain contact with the child when that parent's actions resulted in a PPO? How a PPO affects a stepparent adoption is unknown.

KEY TAKEAWAYS

- The purpose of the Adoption Code is to focus on <u>permanency, stability, and the best interests of the child.</u>

- Even if a putative father is deemed a <u>do-nothing father,</u> many trial courts will erroneously allow a competing paternity case to proceed.

- Trial courts rarely find that MCI's decision was <u>arbitrary and capricious,</u> unless the information provided by MCI was known to be false or misleading.

- Poor word choice in the stepparent adoption provision has created many uncertainties.

- <u>Adoption cases have the highest priority on trial court dockets;</u> they should not be delayed for any other types of cases, even a competing paternity action.

RESOURCES FOR CHAPTER TEN

STEPPARENT ADOPTION

In re AGD, 327 Mich App 332; 933 NW2d 751 (2019).

In re AJR, 496 Mich 346; 852 NW2d 760 (2014).

In re S.M.N.E., 264 Mich App 49; 689 NW2d 235 (2004).

MCL 710.51(6).

SECTION 39 ADOPTIONS

In re LMB, unpublished order of Supreme Court, issued June 6, 2019 (Docket 157903).

In re MKK, 286 Mich App 546; 781 NW2d 132 (2009).

In re MGR, 504 Mich 852; 916 NW2d 662 (2018).

MCL 710.39.

MCL 722.717.

SECTION 45 APPEAL OF MCI DENIAL OF CONSENT

In re OFF, unpublished per curiam opinion of Court of Appeals, issued January 21, 2021 (Docket No. 354195).

In re RC, unpublished per curiam opinion of Court of Appeals, issued October 17, 2019 (Docket Nos. 345959 and 346102).

MCL 710.45.

ADOPTION CODE KEY PROVISIONS

MCL 710.21(a).

MCL 710.25.

ADDITIONAL RESOURCES

Speaker Law Firm, *The Adoption Appeals Guide* <https://bit.ly/3vdI0EX> (accessed June 11, 2021).

Donna Medina and Liisa Speaker, *Adoption Practice Tips* <https://bit.ly/2VSK4X1> (accessed July 17, 2021).

CHAPTER ELEVEN

REVOCATION OF PATERNITY

Complicated Law Generates Many Issues

THE PURPOSE OF REVOCATION OF PATERNITY

The Revocation of Paternity Act provides a way to revoke a man's legal parental status when he is not the child's biological father, making way for the child to have a legal relationship with the biological father. The Act was created to update Michigan's paternity law and address the fact that more children are born out of wedlock, and that there are biological fathers who want relationships with their children.

QUICK LEGAL SUMMARY OF REVOCATION OF PATERNITY

There are four types of legal fathers whose rights can be revoked to make way for another man to be declared the father. There is a different set of requirements for each type of legal father:

- Affiliated fathers establish paternity through an order of filiation. Their paternity can be revoked if it is shown that the affiliated father failed to participate in the court proceedings that resulted in that order.

- Acknowledged fathers establish paternity through an acknowledgment of parentage. Their paternity can be revoked by proof of mistake, newly discovered evidence, fraud, misrepresentation or misconduct, or duress in signing the acknowledgment.

- Genetic fathers establish paternity solely through DNA testing under the Paternity Act, the Summary Support and Paternity Act, or the Genetic Parentage Act. Their paternity can be revoked by showing that the genetic test was inaccurate, the man's genetic material was not available to the child's mother, or a man with identical DNA is the child's father.

- Presumed fathers establish paternity by being married to the mother when the child was conceived or born. There are a variety of ways to revoke a current or former husband's paternity, as summarized in the chart below.

WHO IS SEEKING REVOCATION?	WHAT ARE THE REQUIREMENTS?
Mother	1. The presumed father, the alleged father, and the child's mother at some time *mutually and openly acknowledged* a biological relationship between the alleged father and the child; 2. The presumed father, having the ability to support or assist in supporting the child, has failed or neglected, without good cause, to provide *regular and substantial support* for the child for a period of two years or more before the filing of an action or, if a support order has been entered, has failed to substantially comply with the order for a period of two years or more before the filing of the action; or 3. The child is less than three years old, and the presumed father lives separately and apart from the child.
Presumed Father	1. The child is less than three years old; or 2. The issue is raised in the presumed father's action for divorce or separate maintenance from the mother.

Alleged Father	Either of the following: 1. The alleged father did not know or have reason to know that the mother was married at the time of conception and one of the following: 2. The presumed father, the alleged father, and the child's mother at some time *mutually and openly acknowledged* a biological relationship between the alleged father and the child; 3. The presumed father, having the ability to support or assist in supporting the child, has failed or neglected, without good cause, to provide *substantial and regular support* for the child for a period of two years or more before filing of the action, or if a support order has been entered, has failed to substantially comply with the order for a period of two years or more before the filing of an action; or 4. The child is less than three years of age, and the presumed father lives separately and apart from the child. 5. The mother was not married at the time of conception.

Department of Health and Human Services	1. The child is being supported *in whole or in part* by public assistance; and 2. The presumed father has failed to support the child for two years; or 3. The presumed father lives separately and apart from the child.

Typically, any motion to revoke paternity must be filed before the child turns three years old (except for husbands raising paternity issues in their divorce cases). A trial judge may extend the three-year period for good cause.

In any revocation case, the trial judge can deny a request to revoke paternity if doing so is not in the child's best interests. The best-interest factors the trial judge may consider include the "nature of the relation-

> *In any revocation case, the trial judge can deny a request to revoke paternity if doing so is not in the child's best interests.*

ship between the child and the presumed or alleged father," the age of the child, the harm that may result to the child by revoking paternity, and other equitable considerations "arising from the disruption of the father-child relationship."

PRACTICE TIP: *Standing is important when an alleged father is the one seeking revocation of paternity. Examine whether the alleged father knew or had reason to know the mother was married. If so, and if you represent the mother or the legal father, consider a motion to dismiss based on that lack of standing.*

PROBLEM AREAS IN REVOCATION OF PATERNITY DECISIONS

The Revocation of Paternity Act, passed in 2012, is still relatively new, yet it has already undergone substantive revisions. As revealed in the quick legal summary, the statute is complex and has many facets to prove, depending on what type of father the child has and who is filing the motion. Despite the statute's short history, there are numerous published cases on it, but as with the statute, they, too, are confusing and complex.

THE NEED FOR AN EVIDENTIARY HEARING UNDER THE REVOCATION STATUTE

In *Parks v Parks,* the child was born during the marriage. The couple divorced and shared custody of the child. A couple of years later, a private DNA test showed that the mother's new husband was the child's father. She filed a motion to revoke her ex-husband's paternity. In response, the ex-husband (presumed father) filed a motion for sole legal and physical custody of the child. He denied that he ever acknowledged the biological relationship between the other man and the child, saying he had only recently discovered he was not the child's biological father and the mother never identified the other man as the child's father. Without an evidentiary hearing, the trial judge denied the mother's requested relief and kept the ex-husband's legal parental rights intact. The mother appealed.

The Revocation of Paternity Act does not indicate whether an evidentiary hearing is necessary to establish whether the child was born out of wedlock. The Court of Appeals held that the trial judge is not required to hold an evidentiary hearing unless the moving party first establishes the threshold under the Act—that is, "there are contested factual issues that must be resolved in order for the trial court to make an informed decision." In *Parks*, the mother failed to meet that threshold requirement. She was required to prove that she, her husband, and the alleged father had mutually and openly acknowledged the biological relationship. Her motion did not indicate how she intended to do that. Instead, when she told the presumed father he was not the child's biological father, he filed for divorce and talked to his attorney, his sister-in-law, and his parents about the situation. The Court of Appeals held that the mother's allegations "do not even come close to meeting the 'mutual and open acknowledgment' requirement under the RPA." None of the husband's statements acknowledged the alleged father's paternity but rather merely questioned his own paternity. Nor were the acknowledgments mutual. The trial judge was correct in denying the mother an evidentiary hearing because—even accepting all of the mother's statements—she failed to raise a question regarding whether there was a mutual acknowledgment of the alleged father's biological relationship to the child.

> **PRACTICE TIP:** *If there are disputed facts around whether the mother or alleged father can establish their standing to request revocation, these should be addressed early in the case, before the trial judge hears evidence related to the best-interest factors. You may need to request an evidentiary hearing on the threshold issue of standing.*

THE ALLEGED FATHER'S STANDING TO REVOKE PATERNITY REQUIRES CLEAN HANDS

In *Grimes v Hook-Williams*, the mother was married when she became pregnant with another man's child. The biological father sought to establish paternity under the Revocation of Paternity Act. The trial judge rejected his request because "no reasonable person could have concluded that the plaintiff 'did not know or have reason to know that the mother was married at the time of conception.'" Since the father knew the mother was married, he lacked standing under the Revocation of Paternity Act. The Court of Appeals affirmed the trial judge's decision.

THE ALLEGED FATHER'S ABILITY TO INTERVENE IN THE DIVORCE CASE

In *Boyd v Friskey*, a child was born while the mother and husband were married, but during the divorce it was revealed that another man was the biological father. The mother asked the judge to name the alleged father as the legal father, and the trial judge signed an order allowing the alleged father to intervene in the divorce action under the Act. However, the complaint was dismissed because the mother and husband reconciled. The Court of Appeals held that the alleged father was not legally entitled to intervene in the divorce because "the only parties to a divorce action are the two people seeking dissolution of their marriage." Following the standard in *Killingbeck v Killingbeck*, the Court of Appeals stated that the biological father's "sole recourse was a separate paternity or [Revocation of Paternity Act] action; he was not entitled to intervene in the divorce action."

KAREN'S STORY:
Trying to Make a Family with Her Daughter's Father

Because Karen was married when she became pregnant by another man, the child was legally her husband's. After the divorce, Karen and her child's father married and sought to revoke the husband's paternity and have the biological father recognized as the legal father. They hoped to recognize the family they had created—a child being raised by her two parents. The trial judge said no, concluding that the divorce finalized who the father was for all time.

At the time of the judge's decision, her child was very young and lived with her two biological parents but was required to have parenting time with her mother's ex-husband, who had moved out of state. It was very confusing for her. The relationship with Karen's ex-husband deteriorated further. It took an appeal to finally revoke the ex-husband's paternity.

In the end, Karen and the child's father forged an even closer bond with each other and with their child. They did their best to support their child in a very confusing situation. Even though her ex-husband treated her child kindly, the visitations still impacted the child, who needed to see a child psychologist.

The Revocation of Paternity Act represents an entirely new statutory creation, but many judges could not get past the old way of doing things. This resulted in decisions completely contrary to the legislative intent of the Act: that the "circumstances of the modern family do not fit within the traditional modes of the Paternity Act." It is imperative that judges and practitioners set aside their personal views and look to the legislative intent to properly apply new statutory creations. Failing to do so eviscerates the statute's effect.

—ANDREW COHEN, attorney, Southfield, MI

UNRESOLVED ISSUES IN REVOCATION OF PATERNITY CASES

STANDARD FOR DECIDING REVOCATION OF PATERNITY

The case law in this area is very confusing. In *Helton v Beaman*, the Court of Appeals pointed out that whether or not to revoke paternity is a discretionary matter. Even if a person meets the statutory requirements to revoke paternity, the trial judge can still deny the request if it is contrary to the child's best interests. Because the Legislature did not identify the relevant factors or the legal standard that governs the trial judge's discretion, the Court of Appeals in *Helton* turned to a custody analysis under the Child Custody Act.

Regarding the applicable **burden of persuasion**, the Court of Appeals placed the biological father and the acknowledged father in equivalent litigation postures. It addressed the issue as a dispute between parents rather than between a parent and a third party. This resulted in a presumption in favor of maintaining the child's **estab-**

lished custodial environment. (See chapter 8 re: parental presumptions.) The child had an established custodial environment with the mother and the acknowledged father. To alter the established custodial environment, the biological father needed to present clear and convincing evidence that the change was in the child's best interests under the Child Custody Act. The Court of Appeals concluded he had not done so.

One year later, the Court of Appeals disavowed the *Helton* test in *Demski v Petlick*. The mother in this case had a relationship with the alleged father but then married her husband hours before the baby was born, making him the presumed father. The alleged father wanted to be involved in the child's life, but the mother and her husband deterred him. He filed a petition under the Revocation of Paternity Act and obtained DNA testing confirming that he was the biological father. After a trial, the trial judge found that the child was born out of wedlock and revoked the presumed father's paternity. The trial judge applied the clear and convincing evidence standard to the best-interest factors in the Revocation of Paternity Act. Thus the trial judge found that the child was born out of wedlock and entered a paternity order making the alleged father the child's legal father.

The Court of Appeals disregarded the prior *Helton* decision because *Helton*'s lead opinion was only a plurality decision—no majority of participating judges had agreed on the reasoning in the opinion. Plurality decisions are not binding authority. The *Demski* Court also pointed out that the reason *Helton* looked to the Child Custody Act was due to the then-binding decision of *In re Moiles*, which was later overturned by the Supreme Court. Confusing? Yes, it is. Ultimately, the *Demski* Court affirmed the trial judge because the judge appropriately considered the child's best interests and applied the clear and convincing standard.

BURDEN OF PROVE TO REVOKE

The Revocation of Paternity Act continues to perplex attorneys and judges even on the most basic question: What **burden of proof** must a person establish to revoke paternity? The statute specifically states that an alleged father, mother, genetic father, or acknowledged father must satisfy the statutory requirements by clear and convincing evidence. But what if a presumed father or affiliated father wants to revoke paternity? Does the lower preponderance of the evidence standard apply? The Court of Appeals in *Helton* implied that the plaintiff in a revocation action "has the burden of proving, by clear and convincing evidence, that the acknowledged father is not the father of the child." That language applies to the plaintiff—the person seeking to revoke someone else's paternity, no matter what their role is in the child's life. But this issue could be clearer with the help of the Legislature or the courts.

BURDEN OF PROOF FOR THE BEST-INTEREST ANALYSIS

It is also unclear whether the clear and convincing standard applies to a trial judge's best-interest analysis under the Revocation of Paternity Act. Typically, when a statute does not state the burden of proof, the courts infer that the Legislature intended to apply the preponderance of evidence standard. However, the *Demski* Court accepted the trial judge's use of the clear and convincing evidence standard based on its use in *Helton*. The *Demski* court acknowledged that the Act did not provide a standard but did not reverse the trial judge's use of the higher standard. Thus, it is still unclear what standard should be used.

KEY TAKEAWAYS

- The requirements of the complex Revocation of Paternity Act vary depending on the type of legal father and who is filing the motion to revoke.

- There are four types of legal fathers whose rights can be revoked under the Act—affiliated fathers, acknowledged fathers, genetic fathers, and presumed fathers.

- In any revocation case, the trial court may deny a request to revoke paternity if it is not in the child's best interests to break the child's connection with the man the child thought was his or her father.

RESOURCES FOR CHAPTER ELEVEN

REVOKING PATERNITY PROCEDURES

Grimes v Hook-Williams, 302 Mich App 521; 839 NW2d 237 (2013).

In re Moiles, 303 Mich App 59 840 NW2d 790 (2013) (rev'd in part 495 Mich 944; 843 NW2d 220 (2014)).

Parks v Parks, 304 Mich App 232; 850 NW2d 595 (2014).

Sprenger v Bickle, 307 Mich App 411, 861 NW2d 52 (2014).

Burnett v Ahola, 501 Mich 1055; 909 NW2d 827 (2018).

Burnett v Ahola, 503 Mich 941; 921 NW2d 535 (2019).

Burnett v Ahola, 504 Mich 1002; 934 NW2d 266 (2019).

Demski v Petlick, 309 Mich App 404; 873 NW2d 596 (2015).

Helton v Beaman, 304 Mich App 97; 850 NW2d 515 (2014).

Killingbeck v Killingbeck, 269 Mich App 132; 711 NW2d 759 (2005).

MCL 722.1433.

MCL 722.1437.

MCL 722.1438.

MCL 722.1439.

MCL 722.1441.

MCL 722.1443.

RELATED LEGAL PRINCIPLES

Boyd v Friskey, unpublished per curiam opinion of Court of Appeals, issued February 28, 2019 (Docket No. 341660).

Burns v Olde Disc Corp, 212 Mich App 576; 538 NW2d 686 (1995).

In re Moss, 301 Mich App 76; 836 NW2d 182 (2013).

CHAPTER TWELVE

TERMINATION OF PARENTAL RIGHTS

How to Protect the Parent's Constitutional Rights

THE PURPOSE OF TERMINATION OF PARENTAL RIGHTS

The purpose of child welfare laws is to keep children safe if the parents are unable to care for them or if they have been abused or neglected by their parents.

QUICK LEGAL SUMMARY OF TERMINATION OF PARENTAL RIGHTS

Child Protective Services (CPS) investigates all allegations that a parent has abused or neglected his or her child. If CPS believes that

The purpose of child welfare laws is to keep children safe if the parents are unable to care for them or if they have been abused or neglected by their parents.

the child is in danger, then the Department of Health and Human Services (DHHS) can file a child-protective petition. Most of the time, the child is removed from the parent's home, but sometimes DHHS can develop a safety plan to keep the child and parent together in the same home.

The trial judge or a jury (this is the only kind of child-related proceeding that has a jury) can decide whether there are grounds to take jurisdiction over the child—this is called the adjudication. Typically, jurisdiction is appropriate if DHHS can prove by a preponderance of the evidence that:

- the parent neglected to provide the child with the necessary support, education, medical, or other care;

- the child was subjected to a substantial risk of harm to his or her mental well-being;

- the parent left the child without proper care or custody; or

- the child's home environment was unfit due to neglect, cruelty, drunkenness, criminality, or depravity of the parent.

Rather than going through an adjudication trial, most parents take a plea allowing the court to take jurisdiction, which enables them to receive services to reunify with their children. Services typically include parenting classes, drug testing, Alcoholics Anonymous and Narcotics Anonymous meetings, domestic violence classes, and supervised parenting time.

If, however, the adjudication is based on aggravated circumstances (for example, death to another child, severe injury to the child, abandonment), then the trial judge can move directly to terminate the parents' rights.

If there are aggravated circumstances, or if a parent does not benefit from the services in an nonaggravated case, then the case moves to the termination phase. At that point, the trial judge must find at least one of more than twenty statutory grounds to terminate parental rights by clear and convincing evidence, such as the following:

- The parents physically injured or sexually abused the child or a sibling.

- The parent failed to protect the child from physical or sexual abuse by another person.

- The parent failed to provide proper care and custody to the child.

- There is a reasonable likelihood that the child will be harmed if the child is returned to the parent's home.

If DHHS has proven a statutory ground to terminate, then the trial judge must consider whether termination is in the child's best interests by a preponderance of the evidence. Some of the factors the trial judge may consider are the child's bond to the parent; the parent's parenting ability; the child's need for permanency, stability, and finality; the advantages of a foster home over the parent's home; and the child's placement with relatives as a reason not to terminate parental rights.

Given the fundamental rights at stake in cases involving foster care, it's crucial that judges follow the law. If they don't, it increases the likelihood that children will be unnecessarily separated from their families, which will cause a lifetime of trauma, pain, and suffering.

—**VIVEK S. SANKARAN**, attorney and clinical professor of law, University of Michigan Law School

PROBLEM AREAS IN TERMINATION OF PARENTAL RIGHTS DECISIONS

ADJUDICATION PROBLEMS

WHEN A PARENT TAKES PLEA TO JURISDICTION

Even when a parent wants to plead to the jurisdiction, essentially agreeing they are currently unfit, the trial judge must ensure that the evidence supporting that plea relates to one of the statutory grounds for jurisdiction. For example, it is not enough for the parent to admit to using illegal drugs to prove criminality in the home. Jurisdiction requires that the parent either used drugs in their child's presence or that their drug use impacted their ability to care for their children.

In addition, the trial judge must make sure that the parent understands not only what they are pleading to but that the plea could be used against them later at the termination stage. In *In re Ferranti*, the parents had several children together, one of whom (JF) had spina bifida and required frequent medical care. DHHS filed a petition to remove JF from her parents' care, alleging a failure to "adequately attend to JF's medical needs." DHHS's petition alleged that the parents missed medical appointments and failed to keep her prescription medication refilled. The clutter in the parents' home also made it difficult for a wheelchair to maneuver. At a preadjudication hearing, the parents admitted that they were not refilling JF's medication, even those available at no cost. In taking the parents' pleas, the trial judge "did not advise them that they were waiving any rights. Nor did the court advise them of the consequences of their pleas, as required by the court rules." The trial judge also failed to advise the parents that they could appeal the decision to take jurisdiction over JF. The parents' rights were terminated, but the Supreme Court vacated that decision.

> **PRACTICE TIP:** *As a parent's attorney, make sure you know the status of any related criminal matters before allowing your client to take a plea to jurisdiction. If possible, negotiate to plead to grounds unrelated to the pending criminal action to avoid any admission that could hurt their criminal defense.*

JURISDICTION BASED ON ONLY ONE PARENT'S CONDUCT

If one parent has abused or neglected the child, resulting in a child-protective proceeding, then the trial judge should immediately place the child with the noncustodial parent. For a long time, trial judges around the state would take jurisdiction based on one parent's conduct and jurisdictional plea but then subject the noncustodial parent to all the service requirements (including supervised parenting time with the child) even though the noncustodial parent had done nothing to bring the child under the jurisdiction of the court. This "one-parent doctrine" violated the constitutional rights of many noncustodial parents, ultimately resulting in the termination of their parental rights. The Michigan Supreme Court finally fixed this constitutional problem in *In re Sanders*, 495 Mich 394, when it found the one-parent doctrine unconstitutional and instructed trial judges to honor the due process rights of noncustodial parents.

There were untold victims of the one-parent doctrine (parents and children) during the twelve years that it was used in Michigan. However, one father was able to get his rights back after the trial judge terminated them. In *In re Farris*, the mother had four children: one by her ex-husband and three younger children by her boyfriend. The youngest two children were medically fragile, which resulted in a child-protective proceeding based on medical neglect. As was the pattern at the time, the nonrespondent father of the oldest child was brought into the case as well. The mother entered a plea to the jurisdiction. Even though there were no allegations against the father, nor did he give a plea, the oldest child was placed into foster care, and both parents were made to do a variety of "services." When the nonrespondent father was unable to meet all of DHHS's demands, the trial judge terminated his parental rights (and the rights of the mother and the father of the three younger children). The Court of Appeals affirmed the termination, but Judge Douglas Shapiro wrote a vigorous dissent challenging the use of the one-parent doctrine to terminate the rights of the nonrespondent parent. The case went to the Michigan Supreme Court. While pending, that Court decided *In re Sanders* and remanded *Farris* to the trial court for reconsideration based on that opinion. This allowed the father and his son to be reunified after over 1,400 days apart.

ADJUDICATION OVER SIBLINGS WITH DIFFERENT ISSUES

Sometimes the trial judge has grounds to take jurisdiction based on a parent's abuse or neglect of one child, but those grounds do not justify adjudication over all the parent's children. In *In re Churchill/ Belinski*, the mother was working with her younger child, OTC, on gender reassignment therapy, based on OTC's comments expressing a desire to be a girl. Even though the mother knew OTC was no longer interested, she "grossly overreacted" and "attempted to force a female gender identity" on OTC. The trial judge assumed jurisdiction over OTC and the mother's two older children, SLB and JWC. In an order, the Supreme Court reversed the part of the Court of Appeals's decision affirming the trial judge's exercise of jurisdiction over the older children and vacated the orders of adjudication and disposition for these children because there was no "independent basis to conclude that SLB or JWC came within the statutory requirements of the Juvenile Code, and the petitioner did not present a theory of anticipatory neglect to the jury or to the Court of Appeals."

In re Kellogg involved a parent with two children: DF, who was twelve years old, and JK, who was three years old. The parent had a volatile and difficult relationship with the older child. DF had been removed from the parent's home due to "mental injury" from 2008 until 2017. Most of the allegations in the CPS petition involved the older child. The parent "aggressively" yelled at DF for breaking the rules; DF lived in a "state of fear and anxiety" due to "yelling, harsh punishment, and unpredictable and inconsistent punishment." In contrast, the CPS petition alleged very few facts related to JK, only that the parent had "been observed by professionals to become verbally aggressive with [JK] and unable to regulate her emotional state when responding to him." At a bench trial, DHHS presented evidence about the parent's "overall mental health" because the parent "was yelling and swearing at JK, was neglecting JK's educational needs, had failed to provide JK with consistent rules and with a routine and structure, and had some difficulty managing JK's wants and controlling him." Even though the CPS case focused on DF, the trial judge took jurisdiction over both children.

The Court of Appeals reversed the adjudication as to JK. In combing through the record, the Court of Appeals found no evidence of physical violence as to JK. There was no evidence that the parent's yelling or intimidating stance negatively affected the younger child other than one time when the child flinched. That evidence did not demonstrate a substantial risk to JK's mental well-being for the trial judge to take jurisdiction. In addition, the evidence regarding the parent's "inconsistent rules and lack of routine or structure" focused primarily on the older child, DF. Regarding JK, there was only generic testimony that children do better when they have consistent rules and structure. The Court of Appeals noted that parents are "allowed to have some difficulties managing the wants of and controlling their children." More is required to demonstrate a basis for jurisdiction under the Juvenile Code.

REASONABLE EFFORTS PROBLEMS

IMMEDIATE TERMINATION WITHOUT AGGRAVATED CIRCUMSTANCES

DHHS and trial judges often treat cases as involving "aggravated circumstances" even when the facts do not satisfy the statute's definition. Immediate termination is only available if the parent's conduct amounted to "aggravated circumstances," such as murdering another child, sexual abuse by penetration, severely injuring a child, or torturing a child. The court rules say the trial judge must make a finding within sixty days after the child is removed from the home that either CPS made reasonable efforts to keep the child in the home or that those reasonable efforts are not required due to aggravated circumstances. Unfortunately, many times DHHS, the prosecutor, and the trial judge plow forward as if the case had aggravated circumstances without ever going through the process to make the required findings. The court forms have a line item where the judge can "check the box" if the judge finds there are aggravated circumstances and state the findings that support the identification. Trial judges are not properly completing the forms as it pertains to aggravated circumstances but then allowing DHHS to move directly to termination of a parent's rights without providing any services.

A recently published Court of Appeals opinion and a preemptory order by the Supreme Court both highlight this error. In *In re Sanborn*, the mother "lacked the requisite parenting skills and emotional stability to care for the child." DHHS initially offered the mother services to rectify these conditions, but she failed to do so. DHHS sought termination at initial disposition, and her rights were terminated. However, the Court of Appeals reversed because the case did not involve aggravated circumstances, rejecting the holding in *In re HRC* that "DHHS is not required to provide reunification services when termination of parental rights is the agency's goal."

Soon after *Sanborn*, the Supreme Court reversed the trial judge's termination order in *In re Simonetta*. The mother took Norco and used marijuana during her pregnancy, and her baby screened positive for opiates and THC. The trial judge terminated the mother's parental rights. The mother appealed based on DHHS's failure to make reasonable efforts to reunite mother and child, but the Court of Appeals affirmed. It reasoned that reunification efforts were not required because aggravated circumstances existed as the infant suffered "severe physical abuse, loss or serious impairment of an organ, or a life-threatening injury at the hands of respondent." The Supreme Court highlighted the fact that the case did not involve aggravated circumstances such that DHHS could not avoid its statutory obligation to make reasonable efforts to reunify the parent and child. Hopefully, these two cases will cause trial judges and DHHS to observe the statutory requirements in the future.

> **PRACTICE TIP:** *If DHHS and the trial judge are moving straight to termination without providing services, ask the judge to explain the aggravated circumstances that apply. This will create a record for appeal and pressure the trial judge to require reunification services where the facts don't support immediate termination.*

DHHS FAILING TO PROVIDE OR VERIFY SERVICES FOR INCARCERATED PARENTS

It is all too common that a parent is sentenced to jail or prison during their child welfare case. DHHS workers frequently stop making any efforts to assist parents once they are incarcerated, even if they had been working toward reunification with the child and despite the department's responsibility to do so. Instead the imprisoned parent frequently avails himself or herself of the various services offered in prison (AA class, NA class, domestic violence class, and so on), but DHHS will not accept that as a reason to delay the termination trial (or simply to not seek termination).

In *In re Mason*, the father was in prison when his sons were removed from the mother's household. The department service worker failed to provide any services to him while he was in prison, instead only offering services to the mother. The trial judge nonetheless terminated the father's parental rights. The Supreme Court reversed the termination, holding, "The state is not relieved of its duties to engage an absent parent merely because that parent is incarcerated."

Despite the *Mason* decision, trial judges and the Court of Appeals regularly excuse DHHS's lack of effort when a parent is in prison. Many times, the courts find that DHHS's minimal services satisfied its obligation to incarcerated parents and conclude that termination of parental rights is appropriate because the parents did not benefit from those services. *Mason* categorized the lack of services as a violation of the father's constitutional rights, so why is it any different for the imprisoned parents who came after him?

INTERPLAY OF CRIMINAL AND TERMINATION CASES

Sometimes a parent in a CPS case is simultaneously fighting criminal charges arising from the same alleged conduct. Termination cases often move much faster than criminal cases. This interplay of a criminal case and the child welfare case creates problems because even if the parent is acquitted in the criminal case, they may still lose parental rights.

In *In re Spagnola*, a father was at home alone with his two infant twin daughters when one of them had a seizure and went limp. The father rushed the baby to the hospital, but the hospital believed the father caused his daughter's injuries by shaking her or banging her head against a hard surface. This is known as abusive head trauma. Many parents and caretakers have been criminally accused of shaking a baby and causing abusive head trauma, even though scientific discussion does not support the theory. Whenever a child has an unexplained head injury, DHHS will also pursue a case of child abuse against the parent. In *Spagnola*, the father's parental rights to both children were terminated based on allegations that he shook his daughter, and he was convicted of child abuse. The Court of Appeals overturned his criminal conviction, but it was too late for the father to undo the termination of his parental rights.

DEMANDING CONFESSION OF ABUSE
TO REUNIFY WITH CHILDREN

In *In re Blakeman*, the parents had four children. The wife also babysat an unrelated toddler. One day, the wife left the house for a short time while her husband watched the children. The unrelated toddler had an unexplained head injury (the husband said the child had a seizure). As a result of that injury, DHHS initiated a child-protection case over the family's four children and required the husband to leave his home. Criminal charges had not been brought against the husband, and he professed his innocence. The trial judge refused to allow him back into his home until he admitted to injuring the unrelated toddler. The Court of Appeals reversed the decision for violating the father's constitutional rights and giving him a "Hobson's choice" to either:

> (1) retract his claim of innocence, admit to the child abuse at therapy as a condition of completing services, and expose himself to criminal liability for child abuse, or (2) maintain his innocence, which would likely result in the termination of his parental rights to his four children.

STATUTORY GROUNDS PROBLEMS

There are thousands of appellate decisions that challenge the statutory grounds for termination of parental rights. Those appeals are very fact intensive, and the judge only needs a single statutory ground to terminate parental rights.

In *In re Mason* (also discussed above), the father was in jail during a CPS case. Due to his imprisonment, the trial judge restricted the father's contact with the children (who had previously visited him in jail) and did not include him in the subsequent court hearings. The father had a right to participate by telephone, but the trial judge never informed him. When his rights were terminated, he appealed the lack of notice in the proceedings. The Supreme Court held that "the mere present inability to personally care for one's children as a result of incarceration does not constitute grounds for termination." Under the Juvenile Code, termination is authorized if

1. the child will be deprived of a normal home for a period exceeding two years,

2. the parent has not provided for the child's proper care and custody, and

3. there is no reasonable expectation that the parent will be able to provide proper care and custody within a reasonable time considering the child's age.

The trial judge failed to adequately consider these requirements by accepting the DHHS worker's unsupported opinion that it would take at least six months for the father to be able to care for children after his release from prison. The judge also failed to consider whether the father would fulfill his duty to provide care in the future.

In *In re B and J*, the parents were living in the United States without documentation. Their two minor children lived with them, along with their adult daughter and her two children. The children were removed from the home, and DHHS sought to terminate parental rights, alleging that the father sexually abused his grandchildren and the adult daughter failed to protect them. The trial judge assumed jurisdiction and ordered DHHS to allow supervised visitation and provide services with the goal of reunification. DHHS made little effort to provide services in Spanish. The three adults were detained by Immigration and Customs Enforcement (ICE) and deported. It was clear that DHHS reported the parents to ICE, yet DHHS sought to terminate the parents' rights based on their inability to provide proper care and custody for the children. The trial judge terminated the parents' rights. However, the Court of Appeals reversed, holding that DHHS was not entitled to seek termination under that provision because the department had intentionally created the ground for termination.

When the state deliberately takes action within the purpose of virtually assuring the creation of a ground for termination of parental rights, and then proceeds to seek termination on that very ground, the state violates the due process rights of the parent.

In *In re Gach*, a child was found wandering outdoors unsupervised with two dogs, wearing only a shirt and a soiled diaper. The police arrived and went inside the home where the mother and the child's half sister were, which they described as having dirt and grime everywhere. The mother had three prior terminations, and one of her children died with suspicious injuries. The father had been sentenced to prison regarding that death, and the mother was charged with felony homicide but not convicted. The trial judge terminated the mother's parental rights on several statutory grounds.

The Court of Appeals reversed the termination on each statutory ground. The trial judge erred in basing the mother's termination on the father's prior abusive conduct because there was no evidence that she was still in a relationship with him. She even stated that doing so would put her children at risk. The lack of supervision should have resulted in services to the mother, not termination. Finally, regarding the mother's prior terminations, the Court of Appeals held that "when a parent has been subjected to an earlier termination of parental rights, [that provision] does not justify the new termination because it cannot be clearly and convincingly proved that the parent had failed to remedy the earlier abuse or negligence that led to the earlier termination." The Court of Appeals said a current child protection case should look at current fitness and not past fitness.

BEST-INTEREST PROBLEMS

TRIAL JUDGES FAILING TO DETERMINE IF A CHILD OR PARENT IS A MEMBER OF AN INDIAN TRIBE

With some regularity, appellate courts conditionally reverse termination of parental rights cases because the trial judge failed to inquire whether the child or parent belonged to an Indian tribe. If the child or parent is a tribe member, the family is entitled to protections under the Indian Child Welfare Act (ICWA), which is designed to keep Indian families intact. ICWA makes it more difficult to terminate a parent's rights to an Indian child. If the trial judge "knows or has reasons to know that an Indian child is involved," the trial judge is obligated to make an ICWA inquiry. DHHS and the trial judge must give notice to the tribe or to the secretary of the interior (if the tribe is unknown) so the tribe can be involved with the state court's child welfare proceeding or ask that the case be transferred to its own tribal court.

In *In re Morris*, DHHS filed a petition because the child tested positive for cocaine at birth and the mother had engaged in prostitution while pregnant. The mother and father both stated they had Cherokee heritage. The trial judge checked the box that the inquiry was made but never notified the tribe or the secretary of the interior of the case. It proceeded to termination. On appeal, DHHS raised the issue about lack of notice and asked the Court of Appeals to conditionally affirm the termination, pending the proper notice to the tribe. The Court of Appeals agreed, but the Michigan Supreme Court conditionally reversed the termination instead, sending a message that the courts and DHHS must comply with ICWA.

TRIAL JUDGES FAILING TO CONSIDER RELATIVE PLACEMENT AS A REASON NOT TO TERMINATE PARENTAL RIGHTS

The Court of Appeals in *In re Olive/Metts* conditionally reversed a termination of parental rights because the trial judge did not consider whether the child's placement with a relative was a reason not to terminate parental rights. According to the Court of Appeals, the fact that the children are in the care of a relative at the time of the termination hearing is an "explicit factor to consider in determining whether termination was in the children's best interests." Therefore when a trial judge fails to "explicitly address whether termination is appropriate in light of the children's placement with relatives," the Court of Appeals must remand the case because the factual record is inadequate for the trial judge to have made a best-interest determination. After the *Olive/Metts* decision, there have been numerous conditional reversals, remanding cases to the trial judges to determine whether the child's placement with a relative weighed against the termination of parental rights.

CONSIDERATION OF EACH CHILD'S BEST INTERESTS INDIVIDUALLY

Olive/Metts also addressed another recurring problem in termination of parental rights cases. Very often at the best-interest phase of the case, the trial judge discusses multiple children's best interests all together. Thus the trial judge does not assess the best interests of each child individually—regardless of their ages or other differences among the children. In *Olive/Metts*, the mother had five children, but two of the children were living with a relative. The trial judge failed to consider the best interests of each child individually, resulting in reversal on appeal.

In *In re Farris* (discussed above), there were four children, but Farris was only the father of the oldest child. All four children were placed into foster care because the mother and her boyfriend were medically neglecting the younger children and because the boyfriend tried to strangle the mother in front of the children. However, the oldest son had a different father, and none of the allegations of abuse related to his father. After finding statutory grounds to terminate, the trial judge analyzed the best interests of the four children, saying: "The Court does find, based upon the following, that reasonable efforts have been made and that termination of parental rights of all three parents are in each child's best interest." The trial judge not only failed to consider a single best-interest factor but also failed to consider each child individually (claiming instead that the analysis applied to each child). The prosecutor justified the trial judge's cursory analysis by claiming that because the oldest child was the only child of that father, "the Court's findings were indeed tailored to the best interests of [that oldest child]." Despite this error, the Court of Appeals affirmed the trial judge's decision. Fortunately, the Supreme Court reversed because the father's due process rights had been violated based on the one-parent doctrine (discussed above).

> *The trial judge does not assess the best interests of each child individually— regardless of their ages or other differences among the children.*

A potential end result of a child welfare case is termination of parental rights. If a court doesn't follow the law, it could wrongly—but permanently—deprive parents of one of the single most fundamental constitutional rights. It is the civil death penalty. A court which doesn't follow the law may end up needlessly destroying families.

—**JOSH PEASE,** attorney, Lansing, MI

UNRESOLVED ISSUES IN TERMINATION OF PARENTAL RIGHTS CASES

UNRESOLVED ADJUDICATION ISSUES

ANTICIPATORY NEGLECT AS A GROUND TO TAKE JURISDICTION OVER THE CHILD

While anticipatory neglect is a statutory ground to terminate parental rights, it does not appear anywhere in the adjudication grounds described above. These grounds are written in the present tense, and the Court of Appeals has held that they apply to the parent's current fitness. Logically, anticipating something that has not yet happened is not current, but future. The trial judge must find a current basis to take jurisdiction. Then the trial judge can terminate parental rights if he or she anticipates the parent will neglect or abuse the child based on past neglect or abuse. In *In re Kellogg*, discussed above, the Court of Appeals reversed a trial judge's adjudication on the grounds of anticipatory neglect. However, the Court did not say the doctrine did not apply at the adjudication phase but found the evidence did not support the application of anticipatory neglect in that case. It appears that the Court of Appeals just assumed that the doctrine applied at the adjudication phase. A future case should challenge an adjudication based on anticipatory neglect.

UNRESOLVED REASONABLE EFFORTS ISSUES

NOT ALLOWING VISITATION AFTER ADJUDICATION

In *In re Laster*, the Court of Appeals announced that a parent who has been adjudicated does not have a right to parenting time. The Court of Appeals relied on the court rule which talks about parenting time at the preliminary hearing and the statute which talks about parenting time during pretrial placement. The Court of Appeals stated:

> There is no indication in the language of the court rule or statute that these provisions are applicable once adjudication occurs, nor should they be, given that once adjudication occurs, the court has facts—proven by at least a preponderance of legally admissible evidence—on which to base an even more informed decision regarding parenting time than can be made at a preliminary hearing.

Once the trial judge assumes jurisdiction, DHHS is obligated to make reasonable efforts to reunify the parent and child unless there are aggravated circumstances. How can a parent and child be reunified if they do not have time together? Parenting time is important for the CPS worker to assess the parent's parenting skills, the child's bond with the parent, and many other facts that are highly relevant to whether or not it is in the child's best interests to terminate the parent's rights. Indeed, the Court of Appeals in *In re Newman* held that denying parenting time could be a violation of due process and federal funding law because "the inability of the department to observe the children and parents together … greatly limited the facts available for the determination of the factual questions before the court, and … greatly increased the likelihood of error as to those questions." This holding should be adopted in a published decision.

UNRESOLVED STATUTORY GROUNDS ISSUES
TERMINATION BASED ON ANTICIPATORY FAILURE TO PROTECT.

One of the grounds for termination of parental rights is a parent's failure to protect the child from another person's abuse. A different ground to terminate is based on anticipatory neglect—that is, the parent has abused one child before, and the state anticipates the parent will abuse another child in a similar fashion in the future. However, some trial judges have melded the two concepts and terminated parental rights based on "anticipatory failure to protect"—that is, because the parent failed to protect a child in one instance, the judge anticipates that the parent will fail to protect another child in the future. (See "Sherise's Story.")

SHERISE'S STORY:
Her Baby Was Injured in Father's Care, but DHHS Took Both Her Kids away

Sherise has two sons, ages eight years and three months. Sherise was at work when the baby was injured while in his father's care. Sherise brought the child to the hospital as soon as she learned of the injuries, but DHHS intervened and took away both children. DHHS and the judge seemed to focus on Sherise's reaction at the hospital, saying that she was not upset enough and concerned that she would allow the father to be in the baby's life. Her older son was sent to his father, whom he had not seen in five years, and that man abused her son while Sherise was waiting for the appeal. At least the baby was safe with her mother, but that did not lessen the pain of separation.

The trial judge quickly terminated her rights, even though she did everything DHHS told her to. Sherise's older son cried when they took him away, but she was only given five minutes to say goodbye to him. Sherise felt like her "whole life was over" but decided she would "fight this until the day [she died]." It took an appeal to vacate that termination and finally bring her babies home.

The baby is now four years old and medically handicapped from his injuries, but Sherise is a nurse and is the best person to take care of him. Her older son used to be a straight A student, but after the trauma of removal, he began to have behavior issues in school, telling the teachers he missed his mom.

This occurred in *In re Miteff*, and the Court of Appeals reversed the termination. In *Miteff*, the mother was married to her husband, and they had a three-year-old son, but the father also had a teenage daughter from his prior marriage. At one point, the teenage daughter threatened to poison her three-year-old half brother, and the father became enraged and screamed at her. The teenage daughter told her mother, and CPS became involved due to the father's emotional and verbal abuse. CPS removed the three-year-old son from the home even though his mother had taken him out of the room when her husband and the teenage daughter were arguing. The trial judge terminated the mother's parental rights to her three-year-old son because she failed to protect her step-daughter from her husband's rage, and therefore the judge anticipated that her husband would one day express the same rage at their son, and she would then fail to protect him from her husband. The Court of Appeals reversed, holding that the trial judge's concerns about the safety of the younger child were "speculative" because there were no allegations that the "child had been directly in danger or suffered any ill effects at the hands of [either parent], merely that a potential existed for [his father] to subject the child at some future time to inappropriate behavior." The Court went on to explain the "speculative nature" of the doctrine of anticipatory neglect when it applied in this context (anticipatory failure to protect). Anticipatory neglect was "not intended to serve as the sole basis for the termination of an individual's parental rights without a concurrent demonstration of parental unfitness." The evidence at trial showed that the mother had "sufficient parenting skills" in spite of "her past alleged failure to protect her teenage stepdaughter from [the father]."

USING DOMESTIC VIOLENCE AS GROUNDS FOR ANTICIPATORY FAILURE TO PROTECT

Anticipatory neglect and failure to protect are both viable grounds for a termination of parental rights. However, the trial judges sometimes employ a different twist on anticipatory failure to protect in cases where the parent is the victim of domestic violence. In these cases, the trial judge says that because the parent (usually a mother) cannot protect herself from domestic abuse, the court anticipates that she will also fail to protect her child from domestic abuse in the future, and thus terminates her rights to the child. This has unfortunately occurred even in cases where the child was never abused, and the mother ended the relationship with her abuser. Until the Court of Appeals or the Supreme Court speaks out in a published opinion against expanding these doctrines, domestic violence victims will be at risk of losing their children.

In *In re Sehy*, the Court of Appeals affirmed the termination of a domestic violence victim's rights. Judge Amy Ronayne Krause issued a concurring opinion, disagreeing with the majority's decision that domestic violence was a proper basis for terminating the mother's parental rights. Judge Krause noted that the effect domestic violence has on the child is a proper consideration when viewed "in context," but the evidence on the record in this case "failed to show that [the mother's] husband ever threatened the children, that [the mother's] victimization itself played any role in her ability to provide proper care for the children, or that the domestic violence had any effect whatsoever on the children at issue in this appeal." Judge Krause further stated that, while domestic violence is a very serious issue and an investigation into the matter should take place, the proper inquiry must be the "actual effect on the children, not the hypothetical effect." It cannot be forgotten that removing a child from a parent "certainly will cause lasting harm, especially if that parent is him or herself being maltreated." Terminating the mother's rights based on her status as a domestic violence victim "is nothing more than punishing a victim for being a victim."

UNRESOLVED BEST-INTERESTS ISSUES

USING PREPONDERANCE STANDARD
FOR BEST INTERESTS OF CHILD

In *In re Moss*, a mother had psychotic hallucinations that she was being told to harm her daughter. To protect her child, the mother checked herself into a psychiatric ward. While at the hospital, she said she had thoughts of killing her child. DHHS filed a CPS case, and the trial judge assumed jurisdiction of the child. But rather than offering the mother services to reunify her with her child, DHHS sought to terminate her parental rights at the initial disposition. The trial judge terminated her rights using a preponderance of the evidence standard for the best interests. The Court of Appeals affirmed, reasoning that once a statutory ground is found, the parent loses their constitutional status of fit parent. Parental rights are protected by the constitution. Parents have a liberty interest in the care, custody, and control of their children. (See chapter 1.) Thus, when the state wants to terminate those rights, it should only be able to do so based on clear and convincing evidence. The Court of Appeals's decision in *In re Moss* violates that principle. This issue has not yet been reviewed by the Michigan Supreme Court.

KEY TAKEAWAYS

- The purpose of child welfare law is to keep children safe if the children have been abused or neglected by their parents.

- Even where a parent pleads to jurisdiction, the trial court *must ensure* that there is evidence supporting that plea that relates to one of the statutory jurisdictional grounds.

- The trial court or a jury can decide whether there are grounds to take jurisdiction over the child. DHHS must provide the parent with services so that the parent and child can be reunified unless aggravated circumstances are present.

- DHHS is required to make efforts to assist the parent even when the parent is incarcerated.

- The trial court must find clear and convincing evidence of at least one statutory ground to terminate parental rights; if proven, the trial court must still consider the best interests of the child.

RESOURCES FOR CHAPTER TWELVE

DUE PROCESS

In re Blakeman, 326 Mich App 318; 926 NW2d 326 (2018).

In re Newman, unpublished per curiam opinion of Court of Appeals, issued September 29, 2016 (Docket Nos. 329063 and 320976).

Troxel v Granville, 530 US 57; 120 S Ct 2054; 147 L Ed 2d 49 (2000).

MCL 712A.13(a).

MCR 3.965(c).

ADJUDICATION

In re Adrianson, 105 Mich App 300; 306 NW2d 487 (1981).

In re Churchill/Belinski, 503 Mich 895; 923 NW2d 885 (2019).

In re CR, 250 Mich App 185; 646 NW2d 506 (2002).

In re Deng, 314 Mich App 615; 887 NW2d 445 (2016).

In re Farris, unpublished per curiam opinion of Court of Appeals, issued August 8, 2013 (Docket No. 311967), rev'd 497 Mich 959; 858 NW2d 468 (2015).

In re Ferranti, 504 Mich 1; 934 NW2d 610 (2019).

In re Kellogg, 331 Mich App 249; 952 NW2d 544 (2020).

In re Laster, 303 Mich App 485; 845 NW2d 540 (2013).

In re Sanders, 495 Mich 394; 852 NW2d 524 (2014).

People v Tennyson, 487 Mich 730; 790 NW2d 354 (2010).

MCL 712A.2(b).

REASONABLE EFFORTS

In re HRC, 286 Mich App 444; 781 NW2d 105 (2009).

In re Mason, 486 Mich 142; 782 NW2d 747 (2010).

In re Morris, 491 Mich 81; 815 NW2d 62 (2012).

In re Sanborn, unpublished per curiam opinion of Court of Appeals, issued May 13, 2021 (Docket Nos. 354915 and 354916).

In re Simonetta, ___ Mich ___; ___ NW2d ___ (2021) (Docket No. 162710).

MCL 712A.19(a).

MCR 3.965(C)(4).

STATUTORY GROUNDS

In re B and J, 279 Mich App 12; 756 NW2d 234 (2008).

In re Gach, 315 Mich App 83; 889 NW2d 707 (2016).

In re Miteff, unpublished per curiam opinion of Court of Appeals, issued June 16, 2019 (Docket No. 288265).

In re Sehy, unpublished per curiam opinion of Court of Appeals, issued August 14, 2012 (Docket Nos. 306370 and 306371).

MCL 712A.19b(3).

BEST INTERESTS

In re BZ, 264 Mich App 286; 690 NW2d 505 (2004).

In re Foster, 285 Mich App 630; 776 NW2d 415 (2009).

In re Jones, 286 Mich App 126; 777 NW2d 728 (2009).

In re Moss, 301 Mich App 76; 836 NW2d 182 (2013).

In re Olive/Metts, 297 Mich App 35; 823 NW2d 144 (2012).

In re Vandalen, 293 Mich App 120; 809 NW2d 412 (2011).

MCL 712A.19b(5).

ADDITIONAL RESOURCES

People v Spagnola, unpublished per curiam opinion of Court of Appeals, issued March 8, 2018 (Docket No. 330382).

Speaker Law Firm, *10 Things You Should Know if Your Child Welfare Client is Facing an Appeal* <https://bit.ly/3cSSC63> (accessed June 11, 2021).

CONCLUSION

As you can see from the variety of cases covered in this book, there are many mistakes that judges make that directly affect children. Even though those mistakes may eventually be reversed or vacated on appeal, judges should be aware of the impact their decisions have on the families before them—particularly when judges don't follow the law. It is important for family law attorneys to try and educate the judges about relevant law, encouraging them to learn from earlier decisions and correctly apply the law. Not only will this reduce the need for appeals, but it

> *Judges should be aware of the impact their decisions have on the families before them— particularly when judges don't follow the law.*

will better serve the best interests of the children of this state. Judges who make decisions based on feelings or instinct—without regard to the statutes, court rules, and case law governing the issues—are not acting in the children's best interests, even if they think they are doing the right thing or ruling for the "right" party. By following the law, judges not only show respect for the rule of law but also honor families and their children.

TAKING THE NEXT STEP

When I began writing this book, my purpose was to shine a light on the systemic problem of judges not following the law in child-related cases. But shining a light is not enough. We need a change. A change in how judges decide family law cases to ensure that trial judges are following the law. A change in how appellate judges review family law appeals so that legal errors are not ignored under the guise that it was a "harmless error." A change in how we appoint judges to vacant seats on the family law bench so that the governor will know when a family law seat needs to be filled. A change in how we elect judges by modifying the legislation so that judges with family law experience will fill those seats. Family law attorneys, you can help in each of these areas. Small hinges can swing big doors.

While children and families are harmed when judges don't follow the law, judges who have been trained in family law are more likely to appreciate those laws and properly apply the laws to the families that come before them. Conversely, judges who don't understand the importance of family law legislation and court rules, who treat the family law bench as the "kiddie court" or a "stepping stone" to the regular circuit court bench, are more likely to ignore the law. When judges make decisions based on their feelings about the parties before them, and without framing their decision using the statutes that the legislature designed to protect children and families, then the ultimate victims are the children who the judges thought they were protecting.

If we work together, we can help children and their families. We can give a voice to the children who have to live with the judges' decisions. If you are ready to make a difference in how we "do business" in our family law system, please visit www.liisaspeaker.com/MyBook.

I look forward to working with you.

All the best,
Liisa Speaker

ABOUT THE AUTHOR

Liisa Speaker is a Michigan family law appellate attorney. Liisa graduated from the University of Texas School of Law, and immediately went into appeals (first in Texas, then Michigan). It wasn't until Michigan, however, that Liisa gained a passion for family law. She founded an appellate boutique law firm in Lansing, Michigan, which enabled her to discover and then pursue her passion for cases involving children.

Liisa has worked on many significant Michigan cases, with a long list of published decisions in the family law arena. She has also worked on many other appeals involving children, including termination of parental rights appeals and adoption appeals. She is a fellow of the American Academy of Matrimonial Lawyers, a prestigious national organization that requires significant family law experience and a national and state examination for admission. Liisa is currently an officer of the State Bar of Michigan's Family Law Section. She previously served as a longtime council member, officer, and then chair of the State Bar's Appellate Practice Section.

Liisa frequently writes for and presents to family law attorneys on important topics impacting children and families. At the onset of the COVID-19 shutdown, Liisa launched a webinar series to help family law attorneys, which is in its third season. And speaking of third seasons, Liisa is also the host of a television legal talk show—*In the Name of the Law*—which addresses a variety of areas, including family law. This is Liisa's first book.

GLOSSARY

Against the great weight of the evidence: not sufficiently supported by the evidence in the record

Burden of persuasion: a party's duty to convince the fact finder to view the facts in a way that favors that party

Burden of proof: a party's duty to prove a disputed assertion or charge

Change of circumstances: a modification in the physical, emotional, or financial condition of one or both parents that justifies the modification of a custody, parenting time, or support order

Clear and convincing evidence: evidence indicating that the thing to be proved is highly probable or reasonably certain; this standard is appropriate if the trial judge's decision changes the established custodial environment

Clearly erroneous: the standard or review that an appellate court applies in judging a trial court's treatment of factual issues; under this standard, a judgment will be upheld unless the appellate court is left with the firm conviction that an error has been committed

De novo hearing: a new hearing of a matter, conducted as if the original hearing had not taken place

Established custodial environment: which parent the child looks to for guidance, discipline, the necessities of life, and parental comfort and does so for an appreciable time, while also considering the age of the child, the physical environment, and the inclination of the custodian and the child as to permanency of the relationship

Friend of the Court (FOC): an official who investigates and advises the court in domestic relations cases involving minors

Guardian ad litem (GAL): a person, who does not have to be an attorney, appointed to advise the trial judge, who makes recommendations about what is the child's best interest

Interim order: a temporary court decree that remains in effect for a specified time or until a specified event occurs

Lawyer Guardian Ad Litem (L-GAL): an attorney who is appointed to advocate for the child; the child's attorney in a custody case

Michigan Children's Institute (MCI): the ward for all foster children in the State of Michigan with authority to consent to their placement for adoption

Peremptory reversal: an immediate reversal by the appellate court without full briefing or oral argument

Preponderance of the evidence: though not sufficient to free the mind wholly from all reasonable doubt, there is still sufficient evidence to incline a fair and impartial mind to one side of the issue rather than the other; this standard is appropriate when both parents share an established custodial environment, and the judge awards joint physical custody

Proper cause: one or more appropriate grounds to reevaluate a child's custodial situation that have or could have a significant effect on that child's life

Sequestered: to segregate or isolate during trial

Standing: a party's right to make a legal claim or seek judicial enforcement of a duty or right

Temporary order: a court order issued while a suit is pending, before the final order or judgment has been entered

The record: the pleadings, filings, transcripts of hearings, and exhibits admitted as evidence before the trial court

www.ingramcontent.com/pod-product-compliance
Lightning Source LLC
Jackson TN
JSHW011932131224
75386JS00041B/1353